The Real Estate Guide to Safety

Unleashing the Power of YOU

By ANDREW WOOTEN, C.P.P.

S.A.F.E. Publishing

Unleashing the Power of YOU

I BELIEVE:

"You will get all you want in life if you help enough other people get what they want." **Zig Ziglar**

By Andrew Wooten

Edited by Leo Ramos and Jane Jerrard

Library of Congress Cataloging -in- Publication Data

A Real Estate Guide to Safety

ISBN 978-0-9841648-0-6

THE END

This may be an unusual way to start a book, but this is an "unusual" book. It's about you, your family, your future, and how you can get more out of all of them by giving more to each of them. I believe that this is "the end," or at least the beginning of the end of negative thinking, negative action, and negative reaction; the end of defeatism and despondency; the end of settling for less than you deserve to have and are capable of obtaining; the end of being influenced by little people, with little minds thinking little thoughts about the trivial that is the stock and trade of Mr. and Mrs. Mediocrity. In short for you it is the end of the world's most deadly disease - the "Hardening of the Attitudes." You were born to win.

AUTHOR'S NOTE

This material was initially written as a support document given to participants after a live seminar. It has evolved into a reference manual that you refer to before going on a listing appointment or conducting an open house. It will give you insight on how to conduct your job safer.

The goal of this book is to share ways you can do your job safer. We will discuss how you can:

Share ways to do your job safely

Share details on what has helped other agents

Empower you to maker safer decisions

If you are buying this book because you have attended a program that I have conducted, you have taken a major step to improving your safety. However, if you are looking for academic chirping that will put you to sleep using words to support the author's ego (and he does have one) you have not found it.

I often say that the information I give is something that your grandmother once said; only I keep my teeth in. My credentials are impressive: yes, I have multiple black belts in martial arts; yes, I am certified by the highest law enforcement agencies in the country; and yes, I have worked with organizations that keep the most violent criminals incarcerated. With all of the defense training and weapons expertise, the most powerful weapon that has saved me many times is a simple rule. What I call the Golden Rule. It has saved hundreds of thousands people across America. It can save you too, if you just listen.

SO TAKE A DEEP BREATH AND JUST REMEMBER

ANDREW'S GOLDEN RULE.

"You are your best weapon, your mind, voice, and body. Listen and trust your inner voice. It is the best weapon you have."

Andrew Wooten

Acknowledgements

It would be impossible to more than scratch the surface trying to acknowledge the many individuals who have helped me throughout the years. I could write a whole book saying thank you to the thousands of people who care about me and what I do. So, if your name is not mentioned, please don't feel slighted.

I want to thank my wife Audrey, who is not just my wife and the love of my life, but also my best friend. I could not have done this without your support!

I have been wonderfully blessed to have the greatest parents in the world. The sacrifices they made were amazing. I thank you and I love you.

Momma Sug (Momma), if it hadn't been for you, I would not have met and married the love of my life. Thank you for talking her into it. If you look up the definition of southern hospitality and charm, you will see a picture of yourself. Thank you for being the matriarch of the family.

Family is very important to me. I have been blessed to have a wonderful extended family, starting with my big sister Goldie. You have always been there for me, from changing my diapers to being at my wedding. Thank you and I love you.

To my daughter, Jessica. I'm so excited about your graduation and working with you to write my next book, *Back Off! The College Guide for Safety*. I cannot express how proud I am of you! You have so much to look forward to in the future.

To Robin Church, who has been instrumental in the organization of the office and the development of this material. It has been a pleasure having you on board; you always have an open door.

It takes a village to raise a child, let me start with my neighbors the Turners. Mr. Turner (the bike man), Mrs. Turner (the soft-hearted one), Gail (the disciplinary), Joyce (the rule maker), I think I gave Joyce ulcers trying to keep me out of trouble), O'Linda (remember pushing the car down the street so our parents did not hear it start?) and Big Mike (who was a grown man but still allowed me to hang around), thank you. You are the best neighbors in the world!

Mr. and Mrs. Covington, who are both surrogate parents and friends, from the days of pantyhose rubbing to standing in at my wedding, words cannot express the gratitude and the love you have given me over the years. I am honored that you helped guide me along the way.

My sisters Jacquise and Rose, thank you for allowing me into the family and taking care of me. You are both role models of character and integrity.

My brothers Robert Grassa, Samuel Mimms and Leo Ramos, true friends who have been with me through the darkest of days and the happiest of times.

It is difficult to walk the path of this life without being fed. To my pastors Dr. Rudolph McKissick Sr. and Dr.

Rudolph McKissick Jr, I thank you for filling my soul with direction and God's purpose. May blessings continue to shower down upon you both.

A special thanks to my friend and mentor Audrey Lackie who started this wonderful journey in Florida. Her smile and spirit are contagious. Thank you for being my friend. (I know it is not easy.)

To Marcus Wally for his recommendation that launched me nationwide. I will forever be grateful for your support, guidance and encouragement.

To Debra Waldman, who did more than just write the foreword for this book, thank you. If you are lucky enough to have her as your friend, then you are truly blessed. The 8x10" will always hang to the right on my desk.

To Tony and Nancy Macolusia, supreme examples of character, integrity and faith. I thank you for the gift of your example and support.

A special thanks to Sharon Hoydich, Pam MacConnell, Cheryl Carroll-Nelson and Bonnie Hendrickson. They are not only clients but also friends.

A big thank you to my partners, The National Association of REALTORS®, especially Charles McMillan, Immediate Past President, Rebecca Daly, Marketing Manager, and Colleen Ryan, Manager, Education Services. Thank you for all your support.

My home team, (N.E.F.A.R.) North East Florida Association of REALTORS®. Leadership starts at the top, and Mr. Glenn East C.E.O. is exactly as his title says - a true Chief Executive Officer. Glenn I have learned so much from you. All I can say is thank you, my brother from another mother.

Joy Huber, Education Director. Joy, they said it could not be done, but we did it. You have not only walked with me, you pushed me and stood up for me. We have been able to touch so many people, and save so many lives, and the beauty is that the best is yet to come.

I am very thankful to all those who contributed to this book. I want to thank every inmate I interviewed and every survivor who shared their story. To everyone who has been kind enough to give an interview, share a story, exchange opinions and donate time to me and this book, I thank you all.

This process of work started when I was five years old in San Diego with an incredible person whose name is Sensei Ed Mayfield. I am forever indebted to you.

To you whom I have not named, you know that this process would not have been completed without you, and you are appreciated more than you know.

Chantel Babb, Director, Education & Events, Denver Board of REALTORS®

Paula Bailey, Education Director, Emerald Coast Association of REALTORS®

Karen Becker, Professional Development Director, Wichita Area Association of REALTORS®

Jodie Cady, Events Manager, Michigan Association of REALTORS®

Sue Clark-Nissen, Chief Executive Officer, Quad City Area REALTOR® Association

Elaine Clay, Bay County Association of REALTORS®

Kristi Coker, Education, West Pasco Board of REALTORS®

Bill Costly, Education/Outreach, Traverse Area Association of REALTORS®

Rebecca Daly, Marketing Manager, National Association of REALTORS®

Debi Dechow, Associate Broker RE/MAX Bayshore Properties

Nicole DeMarco, Committee Meeting Coordinator, Daytona Beach Area Association of REALTORS®, Inc.

Glenn East, Chief Executive Officer Northeast Florida Association of REALTORS®

Barbara Freestone, Senior Vice President, Professional & Business Development, Arizona Association of REALTORS®

Cherolyne Fogarty, President, Walk the Talk Presentations

Rohn Goldstein, Chief Executive Officer, South Metro Denver REALTOR® Association

Clyde Goodbread, Chief Executive Officer, Amelia Island – Nassau County Association of REALTORS®

Lisa Gurski, Association Executive, Gainesville – Alachua County Association of REALTORS®

Bonnie Hendrickson, Education Director, Iowa City Area Association of REALTORS®

Robert Hill, Executive Vice President, Vermont Association of REALTORS®

Sharon Hoydich, Director of Knowledge Services, The REALTOR® Association of Greater Fort Myers and the Beach, Inc.

Joy Huber, Education Director, Northeast Florida Association of REALTORS®

Cindy Hughes, Association Executive, Englewood Area Board of REALTORS®

Gene Jones, Jr., President, Dan Jones & Associates, Inc.

Mia Jones, Florida State Representative

Pam MacConnell, Association Executive, West Volusia Association of REALTORS®

Melissa Maldonado, Professional Development Director, South Metro Denver REALTOR® Association

Lorraine Meighan, Watson Realty Corp. REALTORS®, Ponte Vedra

Jackie Montgomery, Business Partner

Annalisa Moreno, Education & Housing Opportunities Manager, Tucson Association of REALTORS®

Cheryl Nelson, Chief Executive Officer, Iowa City Area Association of REALTORS®

Christy O'Connell, Director of Education & Events, Tallahassee Board of REALTORS®

Cherokee Render, Board of Directors President, Cedar Rapids Area Association of REALTORS®

Colleen Ryan, Manager, Education Services, National Association of REALTORS®

Wendy Sapp, Amelia Island – Nassau County Association of REALTORS®

Maribeth Shanahan, Director, Professional Development Services, Naples Area Board of REALTORS®

Diane Simpson, Business Consultant

Sarah Singletary, Director of Operations and Professional Development, Pensacola Association of REALTORS®

Lynne Stephenson, Owner, Flamingo Travel

Heather Thornton, Director of Education, SouthEast Valley Regional Association of REALTORS®

Debra Waldman, Director, Professional Development, Texas Association of REALTORS®

FOREWORD

By Debra Waldman
Director of Professional Development
Texas Association of REALTORS®

Like many of you, I have attended Andrew's classes and was impressed with his unique and captivating method of teaching a subject that many rank up there with listening to talks about insurance. We don't give safety or insurance much thought until we need it, and because we don't ever think we will need it, we often underestimate its value until it's too late. Training you about how you as a real estate agent can go through your day more safely, and thus more confidently, is not a one-time lesson. Your safety and security depend on you taking the lessons shared in his classroom and within these pages and incorporating those changes into your day-to-day behavior.

After reading the content within, you will understand why many agents who have attended his classes want to return. The reason is simple – you cannot change how you might react in every threatening situation by reading through this book once or by sitting in one class. This book was written with the intent that you would read it all the way through and then review the applicable chapters before you enter into that related situation. With so much to remember as you move through your day, I know slowing down long enough to read a few pages might be asking a lot. But I'm sure those agents who have survived an attack, and those who did not survive would all urge you to take a few minutes every now and then to review the lessons here until they become second nature.

What makes Andrew stand out from many of the safety and security experts is his deep commitment to learning all he can about what makes criminals choose one person over another, what feelings survivors were experiencing right before an attack, and what circumstances can be avoided. By interviewing survivors and incarcerated criminals regularly, he has gained a perspective that few possess. His passion for teaching real estate agents about how they can use the lessons he shares to protect themselves, their loved ones, and their clients, is clear to anyone who has attended one of his classes. I work with instructors every day. There are those who teach for a living, and there are those who live to teach. After reading this book, I think you'll agree that Andrew loves teaching; it is not what he does, it defines who he is.

DISCLAIMER

This book is designed to provide practical information on safety, for individuals in the real estate industry. It is sold with the understanding that the publisher and author are not engaged in rendering legal advice or other legal professional services. If legal or other expert assistance is required, we encourage you to seek the services of a competent professional.

It is not the purpose of this book to reprint all the information that is otherwise available in the form of books, articles, etc, but instead to complement, amplify and supplement other texts. You are urged to read all the available material. Every effort has been made to make this as complete and as accurate as possible.

The purpose of this manual is to educate. The author shall have neither liability nor responsibility to any person or entity with respect to any loss or damage caused, or alleged to have been caused, directly or indirectly, by the information contained in this book.

Table of Contents

Why Safety?

"That little voice said something was not right, but I didn't listen and look what happened to me."

One
Why Safety?

Why a safety book? Because knowledge is power! It is my goal for this book to empower you. This information will provide skills, support and options for dealing with violence in today's world. The National Crime Clock shows you what is happening in America.

Crime Clock

One murder **every 32 minutes**

One violent crime **every 6 seconds**

One robbery **every 57 seconds**

One physical assault **every 7 seconds**

One theft **every 2 seconds**

One burglary **every 10 seconds**

One rape/sexual assault **every 2 minutes**

50 women are victimized by an intimate partner **every hour**

One teenager in victimized **every 19 seconds**

3 people become victims of stalking **every minute**

One child is reported abused or neglected in America **every 35 seconds**

One violent crime is committed against a person on the job **every 19 seconds**

One person is killed in an alcohol-related traffic crash

Below are some incidents I found in local newspapers, but you just have to watch your local news to see how prevalent violence is in our modern society. Incidents like this don't just happen in Florida and they don't only happen to women.

Stories

Agent Found Murdered - The body of 24-year-old M. Moore was found Saturday in a home listed for sale. She was found dead in the vacant house listed by another agent. Police are investigating and are seeking the person who called 911 asking them to check on the person inside the property on Saturday afternoon. It is unclear who the person Moore had arranged the showing for was. Her office said, "Someone phoned Ms. Moore to show a house and they killed her."

Few leads in real estate homicide - "My husband left home and never came back," the 30-year-old mother of two said. "I want to know what happened and why." About 24 hours after Mrs. Smith reported her husband missing to police, his body was discovered in the unfinished basement of a vacant house. J. Smith, 36, a successful entrepreneur and real estate agent, had been shot several times.

Town Mourns for REALTOR® Killed Last Week - Hundreds of people turned out to mourn real estate agent R. Doe, who was killed last week while showing a house. The 71-year-old was found dead in a smoke-filled home.

Agent Murdered - K. Phillips, a real estate agent working in a subdivision was brutally murdered with a knife Sunday. At 1:30 p.m. a couple visiting the show home found Ms. Phillips fully clothed body face down in the kitchen. Police think she had been killed around noon. Police said Ms. Phillips was stabbed 27 times all over her upper body.

Practitioner Assaulted While On Job –A real estate practitioner says she was sexually assaulted Sunday while she was staffing the sales office of a new housing subdivision. The suspect walked into the office, which was located in a model home, and presented himself as a buyer. After looking around, he said the home was too large and asked to see something smaller. The associate took him to see an adjacent property, where the man threatened her with a knife and sexually assaulted her. Police were able to identify and arrest the suspect from information she provided on the prospective buyer card and comments he made to the woman about his sex-offender status.

In researching the hundreds of articles and news stories written about this subject, we found something interesting: In nearly every assault, the victim had warning signs.

Remember Andrew's Golden Rule.

"You are your best weapon, your mind, voice, and body. Listen and trust your inner voice. It is the best weapon you have."

Survivors tell us what they would have done differently if they were given the chance. In most cases, doing the following three things could have made a difference.

These are things you can do on your own, even if your office does not have a formal safety program:

1. Trust your instincts.
2. Trust your instincts.
3. Trust your instincts.

We all want to feel safe, yet many people live their lives totally unaware of how to increase their safety.

Did you know that:

Another woman is attacked every 15 seconds

Another man is attacked every 30 seconds

Every seven to nine seconds another identity is stolen.

We have to be proactive in preventing crime from occurring. Our safety depends on our awareness and crime prevention skills. It is my belief that two out of three properly trained people will successfully deter an assault.

Remember . . . Andrew's Golden Rule of Safety:

"You are your best weapon, your mind, voice, and body. Listen and trust your inner voice.

It is the best weapon you have."

As this picture says, "What matters most is how you see yourself." If you see yourself as someone who can defend yourself, and as someone who is willing to learn and adopt a mindset that will keep you safer in this world, your chances for survival in a threatening situation are greatly increased.

What Survivors Tell Me

The real estate professionals who have shared their stories don't always use the same language to describe circumstances leading up to an attack they survived. Some talk about a gut feeling. Others mention a hesitation or an unexplained fear, even a bad reaction in the presence of a person. These feelings take shape in words I hear over and over again.

"Andrew, I knew that I should not have gone there."

"I knew when I opened the car door. I knew something was not right."

If you have a bad feeling, please don't talk yourself out of it for a sale. Listen to your gut feelings and protect your life.

As part of survivor interviews, I ask them to talk about the four common descriptions for your inner voice. Here is one of their stories…

> *"As I was walking out in the parking lot, I saw a young mother with her children and I thought back to when my children were that age. I just smiled and thought 'whew' when, out of the blue, my stomach tightened up and I became frightened.*
>
> *"I knew I should turn around and go back into the store, but I hurried to my car and just as I was getting ready to open the back door, a man*

appeared, pointing a gun at me. He took my purse and car.

"I had just attended a seminar by Andrew Wooten, and I heard his voice saying listen and trust yourself, but I didn't listen or trust myself and I could have easily been killed.

"So when he asked me about the word 'hesitation,' all I can say is don't hesitate: when your voice talks, listen and trust yourself."

Shawndel Collins

How many times have you walked into a building, met someone for the first time and been overcome with fear or apprehension? That little voice inside you screams, "Something is not right." Folks, listen to it. Trust it, because it may be the only warning sign you will get.

Just think of your own reaction when you are walking out of your kitchen and your child or spouse comes around the corner. What happens? You jump, drop that sandwich, and hold your breath. Now that reaction you just had in your home is the same reaction you will have when someone surprises you in a parking lot.

Mary Jane knows from firsthand experience that intuition can be a valuable tool for survival. She told her husband that a particular customer had made her uncomfortable. Despite her gut feelings, she agreed to show the man more homes. She ignored her unexplained fear based on several circumstances:

The customer was well dressed for their two previous meetings.

He stated he was an attorney.

He stated he would conduct a cash transaction.

Disregarding the hesitation she felt, Mary Jane showed the man five homes during the third meeting. Returning to a home they had previously viewed, he suddenly attacked her, stabbing her twice in the chest and once in the neck. He left her for dead. Barely conscious, she managed to get to a phone and dial 911. Today she is a strong advocate for safety precautions in real estate activities.

The Most Important Skill

The most important self-defense skill to have is awareness. Self-defense is 90% awareness of surroundings and self and 10% physical reactions. By being aware, you will avoid situations that can result in a confrontation or physical danger.

Your inner voice has a heightened awareness of your surroundings, even when you are tired, even when it is late at night or early in the morning, even when you are distracted with a million thoughts and a thousand things you have to do before the day is done. When you increase your conscious awareness of your surroundings, it is easier to hear the inner voice trying to protect you.

Did you see the woman sitting on the curb? Did you see the man leaning against the building? Take a second and look around. Scanning an area, street or parking lot when you first arrive makes you less likely to be selected as a potential victim. The first line of defense against a violent situation is to avoid it.

What to Be Aware Of

What is a potentially violent situation and how can you the real estate professional, avoid it? There are several internal and external factors you should consider in order to increase your safety awareness.

Beginning with external factors, think about your environment. Are you walking or driving? Is the area a new suburban development with many lots still vacant, a mature neighborhood or a densely populated section of a city? Are there people in the immediate area? What is the weather like that day? Are there hedges, vehicles, commercial trash bins, alleys or other areas where a person might hide? Is it day or night? What is the lighting like?

It only takes a few moments to stop, scan the area and assess your environment. This assessment is the first step to increasing your awareness and possibly saving your own life.

Another environmental factor to consider is the level of reported crime in the area. Go beyond what the neighbors say and check with local police or sheriffs for an official report of crime statistics for the area. This information not only helps you assess your safety, but also may be important to the buyer of the house you want to sell.

Internal factors we all need to consider include our physical state, our mind and our inner voice-or what some may refer to as intuition. If you are tired, sleepy, hungry, or have a stiff back, sore muscles or a headache, all qualify as physical circumstances to take into account.

When you are thinking of any one or more of these physical states, you are less likely to be aware of your surroundings. Worries, stress or any mental preoccupation, whether professional or personal, automatically reduces your conscious awareness of the surroundings. Any one or combination of the mental and physical circumstances is sufficient to cover up or mask your inner voice, and put your safety at risk.

Technology is the latest greatest benefit *and* risk to the real estate professional.

Texting or talking on a cell phone, checking email or transmitting documents on a PDA are all activities that require attention. As important as the activity seems to you at the time, is your life more important? The distraction of multitasking significantly decreases your awareness and marks you as an easy target for an attacker.

It only takes a few seconds to scan an area for external factors. It only takes a few more seconds to take a deep breath, clear your head and ask yourself if you are ready to go on with your appointment. If it takes too long, if you have to get yourself "psyched up" to go, then perhaps it would be safer to reschedule.

A walk-through with a potential buyer only takes minutes. An attack that could end your life only takes seconds. This is the time to listen to your inner voice. What is it telling you to do? Do you feel hesitant or have an unexplained fear as you think about the appointment? What is your gut feeling about the person? Every second counts.

What Would You Do?

Internal and external factors are all good and well to talk about, but what does it mean for you showing properties and earning a living? Consider the scenarios provided below and which of the solutions offered best describes what you would do. You'll find the safest solutions provided in Appendix Four.

Scenario 1:

You're working an open house when a middle-aged man and his wife show up to see the home. The following day, they call you and ask to see more homes. After you meet them at a home, they ask if you'll come to their home to assess its value. The possibility of a new listing intrigues you.

As you walk through their home, something doesn't feel right to you, but you can't put your finger on what it is. Everything seems to be in order, so you decide you're just being paranoid. They direct you toward the upstairs bedroom next. What would you do?

a. Dismiss your fears as unimportant (after all, the wife is there), and go on into the bedroom with the couple.
b. Pretend like you have just received a call and must step outside to take the call.
c. Call your buddy and ask him to meet you there ASAP before proceeding any further.
d. Don't go by yourself in the first place.

Scenario 2:

You're a new agent who's been working the phones, and a man calls and asks to see some properties. You meet the client and you proceed to show him several properties. You find it a bit odd that he spends extra time in the smaller bedrooms and he explains he'll have part-time custody of his children. But something just doesn't seem right about his behavior. What would you do?

a. Never have taken him to see any properties by yourself. You should have met him in your office and had him complete a Prospect Identification Form and gotten a copy of his driver's license.
b. Excuse yourself to take a call, and call your office once outside to ask them to run a check on this prospect's phone number.
c. Continue showing him properties; after all, you really need to make a sale, and everybody has their quirks.
d. Jot down the license plate number on his vehicle and pay closer attention to his actions at the next property you show him.

Scenario 3:

You get a call from a prospect who says he's at a property you've listed and would like to see it. Business has been slow lately. You're not far from the address, so you agree to meet him there. When you arrive at the property, you find not only your prospect and his wife, but also a second man with him. You're a little apprehensive about this, but you are reassured by the other women's presence. What would you do?

a. Go on into the house with the three people, reassured by the presence of a woman.
b. Call someone from your buddy list and have a buddy meet you around the corner from the

property, so both of you arrive together. Then have your buddy call your office and talk with someone, making sure the prospects hear your buddy say where you are and what you're about to do.

c. Pretend to call your office and talk with someone, making sure the prospects hear you say that the other person is on their way there and will arrive within a few minutes.
d. Pretend that you have received a phone call from your broker and an emergency has come up. You explain that you won't be able to show them the property until you return to your office first. You apologize; get back into your car, promising to return within the hour, inviting them to wait for you there.

Preparing for Safety

"Somebody once told me that luck is the perfect meeting of preparation and opportunity. I would say: Always be prepared."

Samuel L. Jackson

Two
Preparing for Safety

Are you one hundred percent safe in the way you conduct business now?

Do you believe you are safe because **nothing has ever happened to you**? While you may feel safe, that could be a false perception.

But you have already started taking steps to stay safe. You are reading this book. You may have attended one or more of my seminars. You might even check www.justbesafe.com for the latest safety information for agents every week.

The best information gives you the power to prepare and enhance your safety significantly.

Preparedness Preparedness Preparedness

As stated in Wikipedia, preparedness refers to the state of being ready for specific or unpredictable events or situations. Preparedness is an important quality in achieving goals and in avoiding and mitigating negative outcomes.

Personal Marketing Materials

There are a number of things you can do to increase your safety before you even have any contact with a client. Taking these precautions are vital first steps.

1. **Limit the amount of personal information you share in your marketing materials**. Personal marketing materials are an essential part of any real estate professional's sales kit. However, if not prepared properly, the very same sales tools can endanger your life.
2. **Use your business cell phone number, not your personal cell phone or home phone numbers.** Use your office address rather than your home address. Concentrate on your professional proficiency rather than personal information in newspapers, resumes and business cards.
3. **Your life story is not necessary**. "Getting to know your client" does not need to include personal information about your children or where you live. Be guarded with your personal information. Giving out too much of the wrong information can make you a target. Just as you wouldn't spill your guts to a stranger you just met on an airplane, don't share all that information with a potential attacker posing as a possible sale.
4. **Your marketing material should show a professional, someone dressed appropriately, backed by a reputable company and surrounded by a lot of activity.** You should use a professional photograph, one you would ask your boss to display in the office. Don't appear isolated or

independent: mention your office and company. It's important that clients see you as part of a large group of professionals. This imagery implies you all look out for each other.

Rule of Five

Criminals like the element of surprise. They don't want anyone to know of their plan to hurt you, so one of your best preventive tactics is to let the new client (and potential attacker) know that you periodically check in with others in your office. To do this effectively, you must first establish a protocol for doing this and practice it regularly. A commonly used plan related to the check-in strategy is the Rule of Five.

Remember when your mother said that there is safety in numbers? Well, she was right! There is always safety in numbers.

Create a buddy list. I would suggest a list of five people. Some of your buddies may be agents in your office and some may be agents in a different office. You can also include friends and family members on your buddy list. In any case, whoever your buddies are, be sure to call five people on your buddy list when you are going out on a call alone. Remember: there is safety in numbers.

Why five people? Because people are busy, and the chance of one or more of your contacts being otherwise occupied when you call is pretty high. Plus, people don't always do what they say they will, and your first contact may have had something come up that changed her plans, making her unavailable to any call. Two down, and you still have three other people you can call in an emergency.

Make a regular practice of calling your buddies every half an hour to let them know where you are. If a couple of hours go by and you haven't called in, others will know that something is wrong.

An unexpected property showing is an ideal time to use your buddy list. If you decide to go on an unexpected showing alone, a buddy on the phone is the next best thing. Let your five buddies know where you are going, with whom, and when you will be back. Don't forget to call them regularly. This doesn't have to be a long call; your buddy may pick up the phone and say, "I'm busy; talk to you later." Or you may get her voicemail. You can always pretend that the call is continuing and that your buddy is going to meet you there in a few minutes. Then when you hang up, you can try your next contact. If you need to say something for the benefit of the client who's with you, tell them another call was trying to beep through while you were on the phone with your first contact.

Your Cell Phone = Your Lifeline

Your phone is a valuable tool in this process. As long as you don't use the speakerphone function, people can't tell if you're on the phone with a real person, or talking to someone's voicemail. They don't know if the person on the other end has hung up, so keep talking as though they're there. (Keep your phone on vibrate so it doesn't ring in the middle of talking to your "imaginary friend.") If you're uneasy with someone, excuse yourself and say something like, "I'm sorry, this is my broker…" and continue your conversation. "Oh, you're right around the corner? Okay, I'm going to let them go upstairs and see the bedroom, and we'll see you in a minute." Then walk outside under the pretense of waiting for your broker to arrive.

Suppose you are the buddy receiving the call for help. Call 911 and report your buddy's location immediately, while keeping your buddy on the phone, if possible. Your buddy had already told you the address where she was going to be, so you should have this information handy.

In preparing for your safety, know in advance which buddy you can call that day.

Your cell phone can be your lifeline. This may sound dramatic, but it's true: if you find yourself in a dangerous situation, your cell phone could mean the difference between life and death. Be prepared before you need to use your cell phone. Program your emergency numbers into speed dial. These numbers should include emergency road service, your office, your buddy, and your family numbers. Learn how to use your speed dial before you need it.

Make a habit of charging your cell phone whenever you can-when you get back to the office, during the day in your vehicle or at home in the evening. It should become a part of your daily routine. That way, it will never run out of power at a time when you need it most. Contrary to some beliefs, you do not need to let your phone battery charge completely to maintain its capabilities. Keep a phone charger that can be plugged into the cigarette lighter in your car, just in case you forget to charge your phone overnight. If it's running low on power, at least you can charge it temporarily until you get home that evening. Keep in mind that some chargers only work when your car's engine is on, so you'll need to plug in the phone to get a charge while driving to the next location. If you use a Bluetooth headset or other hands-free device, charge this at the same time you charge your phone.

Wear your cell phone. No, it's not the most attractive accessory, but you should wear your cell phone in a belt holster or on a lanyard around your neck. Your greatest source of help is your cell phone. If you keep your phone in your purse or briefcase, you could be separated from it when you need it the most. If you are in immediate danger, run for safety first, then, when you have the opportunity, call 911. When you have to call 911, stay on the line. Do not hang up. The personnel handling the call may need vital information from you including your location. This is not the movies or television, just because you are calling from a cell phone that has a GPS locator device does not guarantee police can locate you.

In my seminars you will hear me talk about your imaginary friend. When you feel a situation is becoming risky, one option is to have a conversation with your voicemail/imaginary friend while you are walking to the car. Here is an example of how it can decrease the chances of victimization.

> You are leaving your office late one evening, and everyone else has departed. Because you arrive later to work, your vehicle is in the farthest space from the office. As you cross the lot, the hair on your arms stands up and you get a feeling that something is not right. You are closer to your car than walking back to the office.

This is the time to take out your cell phone and have that conversation with your imaginary friend. The conversation might go like this:

> "Hey Mike, you are meeting me at my office? Well, I am in the parking lot close to my car. I'll wait for you here. You are 30 seconds away? Great. See you in a minute."

If someone is lurking in the bushes they have just heard you say someone is meeting you and will be there within seconds.

Dress for Success . . . and Safety

Your wardrobe can improve your safety. We all enjoy choosing an outfit for the day. Looking successful is an important part of being successful in real estate, right? Your image is important, so dress professionally.

However, dress for safety as well. Look professional, but wear clothes that are comfortable and shoes you can run in. How far could you run in those cute little stilettos? It's more likely that you'd twist an ankle and fall. Whether you are a man or a woman, don't wear flashy jewelry. Expensive jewelry can make you a target. We recommend that you save the flashy jewelry for formal occasions. Criminals will scout real estate representatives and homes for jewelry and items that are easy to sell. Thieves often work in teams. So limit your diamonds when you are in the office or on the road.

Dress for the weather. Your mom used to tell you this for good reason. If your car breaks down or you need to escape a dangerous situation on foot, you could find yourself exposed to the weather for an extended period of time. In the winter, bring a coat with you and keep a blanket in the trunk of your car. Plan for the unexpected. Keep a small gym bag in your trunk that has a pair of tennis shoes, a sweater, and a couple bottles of water. You may need to walk some distance, so make sure you'll be able to do that if your car becomes disabled.

Distress Code

Whether you use the Rule of Five or all you have is two, prepare the people you might call before going on an appointment. Create a distress code, an innocuous key word or phrase that will indicate you need help. You and your buddies should agree on a phrase that will indicate to them that you need help, without alerting a client who may be listening to your call. It should be something you wouldn't naturally use in regular conversation, but that wouldn't seem out of place to a client. Here are a couple of examples.

- "I'm at the Jones house and I need the red file right away."
- "I forgot my office keys and I have to drop off a file after this open house. Could you bring my keys here immediately?"

Don't use this phrase casually, as overuse will diminish its effectiveness. You'll become like the boy who cried, "Wolf!" out of boredom, then got no response when a wolf finally did appear. But trust your instincts; don't hesitate to use the signal if you feel uneasy. For example, you may be in your car with a client who is beginning to make you nervous. (You should not have a client in your car to begin with, but we'll get to that in a later chapter.) For one reason or another, you feel uneasy about the person. You do not want to be in an empty house with him.

Call the office, tell someone where you are going, and ask them to pull out the Yellow File. In this case,

Yellow File may be the prearranged distress code to have someone meet you at the site so you will not be alone. You can make up your own distress code, i.e. DOG FOOD (when you don't have a dog) or I'm going to MAYDAY Lane (and there is no Mayday Lane). The distress code should be used if you are uneasy, but do not feel you are in danger. If you are in immediate danger – leave the area and do not hesitate to call 911. Law enforcement officials all over America would rather be proactive than reactive. Authorities agree that most rapists and thieves are looking for easy targets. Be assertive and leave a dangerous situation early. Use your distress code for times you feel uneasy and always trust your instincts. Remember Andrew's Golden Rule: "You are your best weapon, your mind, voice and body. Listen and trust your inner voice. It is the best weapon you have."

What Would You Do?

Let's apply what you have learned so far. In each of the scenarios below, choose the answer that reflects what you would do. Then read the scenario again and choose the answer that reflects what you believe to be the safest solution. You'll find the safest solutions provided in Appendix Four.

Scenario 1

You consistently receive an extremely higher number of phone calls at your office for showings and listings, much higher than other agents in your office. E-mails from your website are also numerous. However, most of these calls and e-mails never materialize into sales. You consistently have a high number of no-shows at the office for appointments that you have made. When you are conducting an open house, your traffic is extremely high, however your sales are far below everyone else in your office. What are the areas you need to look at?

a. Your closing technique.
b. Where you are advertising your open houses.
c. The photograph of you that appears in your ads.
d. Your telephone technique.

Scenario 2

You arrive at a home a prospect has requested to see. This is an unfamiliar neighborhood to you, but it looks nice and quiet. As you go to open the lock box, you feel a cold shiver up your spine but dismiss it as nerves. Once inside the house you begin to do a walk through, looking for interesting things to point out to your clients. All of a sudden you get an uneasy feeling. You cannot pinpoint why, but something doesn't feel right.

What should you do now?

a. Dismiss your feeling, what could possibly be wrong?

b. Call your buddy list and use your pre-determined distress code.
c. Lock the house and leave immediately until someone on your buddy list can join you at the house.
d. Call 911.

Scenario 3

You've recently become engaged. Your fiancé surprised you with the most beautiful diamond you've ever seen! You promised him that you'd never take it off. This afternoon, you are meeting a new client in the office. He's an attractive man who appears to be single, and was quite flirty with you over the phone. You want to establish a professional relationship with him so that you can sell him a house. What's the safest way to do that?

a. Make sure the photograph of you with your fiancé is well in view during your meeting in the office.
b. Show off that gorgeous diamond on your left hand.
c. Refer to your fiancé often in your conversation with the client.
d. Don't be alone with him in the office and introduce him to others.

Scenario 4

This is the busiest day you've had in a long time, and boy, is it welcomed! After dropping your daughter off at school, you have to meet a couple at your office, and then show them a few homes before a luncheon meeting with the local Chamber of Commerce. After the luncheon, you're sitting at an open house for two hours, and then you must head back to the office to meet a new client and assess his needs. Next, you have more homes to show a couple you've been working with for a few months. Finally, you need to stop by and pick up a signature on a new listing on your way home. What should you do before each of the stops in your busy day?

a. Check your voicemail to see if there are any calls you need to return.
b. Call your buddy to let her know where you are going and with whom.
c. Check in with the office receptionist.
d. Update your status on Twitter.

Where Does Crime Occur?

Wherever people are gathered, the potential for crime to occur exists.

Three
Where Does Crime Occur?

Despite common beliefs that the office provides a safe environment in which to work, workplace violence is the #1 cause of death or injury on the job for women, and the second or third leading cause for death or injury for men. According to a recent survey, workplace violence poses the greatest security concern to businesses. And violence on the job is increasing.

Workplace violence, identity theft and other forms of crimes in the office can have a devastating effect on the productivity of a business and its employees. Each year employers report two million assaults in the workplace. Another estimated eight million assaults go unreported. Workplace violence accounts for nearly 20% of all violent crime, costing business owners $36 billion annually.

Every office needs to implement a formal safety program. A good safety program includes basic rules and guidelines, on-going assessments, action plans for improvements, and future goals. If you require assistance in developing your safety program, please contact us at www.justbesafe.com.

CPTED

Our answer to office security is CPTED (Crime Prevention through Environmental Design). CPTED is a new approach to crime prevention. Much more far-reaching than deadbolts on doors or locks on windows, CPTED principles are applied easily and inexpensively. The first step is a risk assessment. This is a valuable instrument that can help you develop new goals and be a safer, more successful organization. It is designed to help your company meet the following objectives:

Identify the assets that need protection.

- Indicate the types of risks that might affect assets.
- Determine the probability of risk/loss at your location.
- Measure the potential impact of risk/loss "in dollar value."

The key aspects of your business will be examined:

- Geographic location
- Exterior and parking area
- Structural details of building(s)
- Organizational and operational aspects of business

Now why do we need all of this? Let's look at the numbers again. A business is victimized every 15 seconds. Now let's look at what is in your office. How many clients' personal information is in your office? What does that information include-copies of driver's licenses, copies of checks, loan applications?

Now let's talk about how to better secure the office. It again starts with a risk assessment tool. Every office is different, but when you look at the cost of being held financially and legally responsible, it's a sound investment. It has been my experience that most offices can be secured with a very minimal investment and with the proper training and accountability assigned to the right personnel.

Office Security-Protecting Your Assets

Most people really do not use the resources that are available to them at no expense. We are so quick to install new locks, cameras and access controls, but do not utilize the internal tool that we already have which is the question of "How easy is it for someone to break in?" The simple answer is:

How many copies of office keys are out?

How many spouses have access to those keys?

What about delivery personnel such as UPS, FedEx? Maintenance and janitorial services?

Is the office ever open at night? If so, can sensitive areas be accessed?

Are all windows that open checked every night before the building is locked up?

Office Safety Protocol

Your formal safety program should include a policy that deters assaults by insisting that everyone positively identify the people you are working with. Brokers should have emergency information for everyone in their real estate office.

It should not only be policy but a routine to know where the agent is going to be so the police can help, should a crime occur, or if the agent contacts someone with a "code red" distress alert.

Meet your clients in the office.

You have heard this stated multiple times; however, it is something that people rarely do. For the few of you who follow the rules, great. For everybody else, follow this example:

> *"I have been a broker for over 20 years and it is a rule in my office that we meet all of our appointments in the office and complete all the necessary forms. It is why I believe we have such repeat business. Clients want and expect professionalism. They do not want to work with someone operating out of the trunk of their car."*

Deidra Johnson, Broker

Prospect Identification Form

Know the clients you are doing business with! Offices across the nation are now asking for photo identification and information from each client before going to view property. Every client who wants to meet with an agent should expect to be asked for identification.

This should be openly obtained, preferably in the presence of an associate. Photocopy the driver's license of a new prospect. Legitimate clients do not mind you copying their driver's license. We freely show our license to the clerk at the grocery store when we write a check and we show our ID to rent a movie. We can and should expect identification from our client before we show a home worth hundreds of thousands of dollars.

Verify the identity of a new client. This means call references, her place of employment and verify her current address. Information should be retained at your office. Knowing that he has to complete an information sheet may be enough to discourage an assailant. The form is quick and easy to fill out and asks for name, address, employer and automobile information. Not only does this procedure identify the person you are working with, it helps qualify a prospect and aids police if something does happen to you.

Using the Prospect Identification Form is a great way to communicate with the office staff. When you and your client leave the office, make a show of sharing this information with someone. If something does happen to you, the information found on the form will assist police in finding you. Victims of crimes can be missing for days before co-workers begin to worry, unless we tell them when to expect us back.

This simple form may be the best preventative safety measure you and your office can exercise. We have found that customers are very understanding of why we need this information. There has been little or no resistance to providing the identification. If a customer does object, that in itself should raise a red flag. (Please visit our resource page at www.justbesafe.com for a variety of downloadable forms.)

Agent Identification Form

If there is an accident or an agent does not check in when he was scheduled to do so, the broker or the police will need this information quickly. We recommend placing the Agent Identification Forms collectively in a separate folder that anyone can access. The information must be updated at least once a year.

Agent Itinerary Form

This simple form helps you find an agent when there is a problem at home and gives you a place to look when an agent is missing. Many agents print out an additional "show list" and attach the form to it. Your front office staff will appreciate having this information if they need to contact an agent.

Working at Night

Preparation, preparation, preparation is all that is required to work safely at night, whether it is in the office or a remote site. This section will talk about the use of law enforcement, and how to use your office staff to reduce the chances of victimization.

Here are some simple steps that can save your life.

1. Walk the entire office with your broker before everyone else leaves, making sure that every office is checked, that every window is closed and locked.
2. Notify local law enforcement that you keep a pot of coffee on until 9 p.m., and ask them to use your parking lot for meetings and writing reports.
3. Make sure you can see your car and surrounding areas. Have night lighting installed, and remember the 3-foot 10-foot rule: shrubs trimmed down below three feet and trees trimmed so branches are not below ten feet.

You may find that a lot of this seems like common sense. Congratulations if you are already practicing everything we have covered. Although logical and certainly based in a common-sense approach to professionalism and safety, thousands of attacks and hundreds of murders still occur in the real estate setting.

Which makes us ask the question: Why don't we all do these things regularly?

Some people may just get complacent, or lazy, or think what my students in the survivors' class say: "I didn't think it would happen to me."

Just as it's easy to let your guard down, it's also easy to fall into certain patterns of behavior. You go to a regular meeting every week at the same time; you drop off the kids at school and pick them up at certain times; you go into the office at a specific time; you leave at the same time every day.

Criminals who are stalking a target watch for patterns in your behavior. They want to know what time you're most likely to be alone, or when they can arrange a "chance" encounter with you to catch you off guard. While we can't control every aspect of our schedules, we may be able to avoid patterns by varying them slightly each day. Take a different route as you drive between destinations, or make an unscheduled stop to run an errand along the way. Arrive at your weekly meeting a little early, but not always the same amount of time early, and make sure others will be there when you arrive. Park in a different area than you usually park. An occasional random variance in your behavior moves you from an easy predictable target to an unpredictable, difficult person not likely to be a target.

Internal Theft

According to the U.S. Small Business Association, almost two-thirds of business theft is committed by employees. The association estimates that more than one billion dollars per week is stolen from employers, and that nearly one-third of business bankruptcies are caused by internal theft.

Understanding common schemes used by employees who steal is the key to developing an internal-theft prevention strategy.

Simple embezzlement: An employee pockets petty cash or fails to return change from a purchase for the company. The employee uses petty cash for his own purposes and fails to reimburse the company.

Pilferage: An employee uses company supplies for personal purposes. She may take pens, paper and other office supplies. In a retail setting, employee might steal merchandise before it even reaches the shelves.

Payroll fraud: Phony names are added to payroll and the administrator collects the salaries.

Computer crime: An employee steals proprietary information from a business computer for financial gain.

Securing Your Home Office

Many real estate professionals do not use a commercial office, but exclusively work from home. Take some simple steps to discourage criminals from choosing your home as a target. Here are ten tips for securing your home office from those who would do you harm:

1. Consider investing in an alarm system if you don't already have one. If you do, make sure you have a panic button feature you can easily use in the room you use as an office.
2. Your home should have deadbolts with full one-inch bolts on all entry doors. These should be installed in addition to existing locksets. If you have a door with glass panels within three feet of the lock, you should have a double-cylinder deadbolt, which require a key on either side so that a burglar cannot simply break the glass and reach through to unlock the door. If a door has conventional glass panels, consider replacing them with shatterproof glass or with polycarbonate material.
3. Secure your windows with locks. You can mount locks on the corners or sides of windows to keep them secure even when partially open. You can also do this with window pinning (inserting a pin or nail above a window so it can't be opened) or track fillers (such as a wooden pole placed into the track of the window).
4. Make sure all porches, entrance areas, and yards are well lit. Turn on exterior lights when you're home at night, plus interior lights when you're away in the evening. You can use timers at staggered times in various areas of the home, even when you're there. That way, the lights are on all the time and it's unclear to burglars whether or not you're there. This will also keep you from walking into a darkened

room when you're at home. Outside, motion-sensitive lights are a big crime preventative measure, especially in the back yard. Criminals don't want anyone to see what they're doing.

5. Prune any shrubbery that hides doors or windows. Remove tree limbs that allow access to reach second-story windows. Remember the "3-Foot, 10-Foot Rule." Keep your yard clear of litter and debris that could not only provide a hiding place for criminals, but also give the impression that the home is unoccupied or the residents don't care about their environment. Degraded neighborhoods with unkempt yards have increased levels of crime.
6. Keep window blinds or curtains closed at night or when you're not home. This minimizes a criminal's opportunity to peek inside and see opportunities.
7. When someone you don't know comes to your door, ask to see his identification before opening the door. You'll need a peephole in your front door or a secure screen or glass outer door for this.
8. When you're out of town, make your home look occupied. Install timers on indoor lights so that they're on in the evening. Instead of stopping your mail or newspaper delivery, ask a trusted neighbor to take care of picking up both every day. Keep a car parked in the driveway. Arrange for someone to shovel snow or mow your yard.
9. At no cost to you, your police and sheriff's department will be glad to help when needed. Call them immediately if you see, hear or have a good reason to suspect that a crime is being committed.
10. Organize a neighborhood watch group and agree to keep an eye on each other's property. Ask people

to call 911 when they see suspicious activity or crimes in progress. Remember that block clubs and neighborhood watch groups are not just for people who own single-family dwellings.

Whether in your company's office or your home office, following these few simple strategies will help you stay safe. Not having to worry about someone attacking you will also increase your confidence and could even lead to more listings and sales!

Securing Your Virtual World

Technology can be used against you by criminals intent on targeting you. In today's online world, threats come from many places, both domestic and foreign, and in sometimes surprising ways. If your computer does not have firewall and virus protection software, buy them immediately and keep them updated.

Ask an IT consultant which software would best suit your needs and get it installed. Do it today. If you have a wireless, DSL or broadband Internet connection, this is even more crucial. Even when you turn off your computer, these connections remain active, and your computer can be taken over to send malicious e-mails containing viruses or other malware, or even as a relay for messages between terrorists!

Viruses that can infect your computer are being devised every day by people who have too much time on their hands. An updated virus protection program is your best defense against them. Set your program up to download updates automatically. Viruses usually arrive as attachments to seemingly harmless e-mails, and may even come from someone you know whose machine has been hijacked by hackers.

Be wary of any attachments. Never open an e-mail attachment you weren't expecting, or from someone you don't know, no matter how funny or inspiring it promises to be. Even if it doesn't erase your entire hard drive, it may install some type of tracking cookie on your computer that will tell someone else what you're doing, and may even record your passwords to access websites like your bank or other private accounts. Chapter Seven of this book goes into more detail about identity theft.

If you have a laptop, be extra careful with it. There are products and services on the market that may help in the security and recovery of your laptop and can even destroy sensitive data stored from a remote location. Rather than endorse any particular product or service, I encourage you to research this if your responsibilities require you to store significant sensitive data such as your clients' personal identifiers, on your laptop or if possession of your laptop would give someone access to data files elsewhere. I recommend using a laptop only for limited tasks, while keeping the main portion of your information on a desktop computer. You may also want to consider using a flash drive that you can keep in a secure place; so none of your data is stored on your laptop's hard drive.

Never leave your laptop unattended. It only takes thieves a few seconds to grab it and go. This includes in airports, coffee shops, during open houses, or when making presentations at meetings. If you must leave it in your car, lock it in the trunk, out of sight, and put it there before you arrive at your destination.

Most thieves know that there's a trunk release switch inside the car that they can use if they merely break a window to get to it.

What Would You Do?

In each of these scenarios, choose the best answer from among those provided. You'll find the safest solutions provided in Appendix Four.

Scenario 1:

The husband half of a couple to whom you've been showing several houses calls you on a Saturday afternoon and says he's at one of the houses you've shown them before. He says his wife was called into work, and he can't remember whether it was this house or another that had the nice workshop off the garage. He would like to take a quick look again. The family that lives in the home now is not at home. Can you meet him there and show him the garage?

a. Tell him you can meet him. Call your buddy list and have someone go with you. Then when you

and your buddy are on your way, call your broker.
b. Tell him you're currently showing property to someone else and offer to meet him in an hour at your office.
c. Tell him you're unable to meet today, and suggest that you meet in your office tomorrow, when his wife is available. Then you can review all the details of the houses you've shown them.
d. Tell him you'll be there in half an hour, and then head out to show him the house again.

Scenario 2:

You're setting up your home office, and look forward to being able to get some work done there without having to go into your broker's office. Which of the following is an element you need to include in your home office?

a. Workspace with desk, chair and sufficient lighting
b. Secure wireless Internet access
c. A secure filing system for your customers' paperwork
d. A reception area for customers

Scenario 3:

While working at an open house where traffic is slow, you're using your laptop to check and respond to emails. You're in the middle of typing a response to a client when someone shows up to see the house. What would you do?

a. Close your laptop and leave it on the desk where you were sitting while you show them the house.
b. Leave your laptop as you were working on it and show them the house.
c. Tell them to look around while you finish, and you'll be with them in a few minutes; take the time to close your laptop and secure it.
d. Ask them to have a seat for a moment while you finish, and hand them a flyer about the house to look at while you close your laptop and secure it.

Workplace and Domestic Safety

"Violence is an unfortunate reality of our times and has far-reaching consequences for both employees and organizations. We may not be able to eliminate violence entirely from our workplaces, but we can take a proactive stance."

Judy L. Jacobs

Four
Workplace and Domestic Safety

I would be negligent in my duties as your safety instructor if I did not mention workplace violence. We all play a role in the detection and prevention of workplace violence. The very nature of our business places us within close proximity to our coworkers. So, we are the first to see the warning signs of workplace violence and we need to know what to look for and how to respond.

Here are a few facts:

- Workplace violence is the #1 cause of death or injury on the job for women.
- Workplace violence cost business owners $36 billion annually.
- More than 40% of the women who die at work are murdered.
- Workplace violence is the second or third leading cause for death or injury for men.

Violence Warning Signs

There is no way to precisely predict when a person will become violent, but there are behaviors that should trigger concern and action from an employer:

- Irrational beliefs and ideas
- Verbal, nonverbal or written threats or intimidation
- Fascination with weaponry and/or acts of violence
- Expressed desire to hurt self or others
- Redirecting blame
- Having a romantic obsession that is not returned
- Fear among coworkers and/or clients
- Drastic change in belief systems
- Displays of unwarranted anger
- New or increased stress at home or work
- Inability to take criticism
- Feelings of being victimized
- Alcohol or other substance abuse problems
- Expressions of hopelessness or anxiety
- Productivity and/or attendance problems
- Violence toward inanimate objects
- Stealing or sabotaging projects or equipment
- Lack of concern for the safety of others

Distraught Clients

> *"Agent Shot at Point Blank Range [July 2008]. When the real estate agent, 33, went into a conference room to meet with his former client, 73, he had no way of knowing what was to come next. The client, allegedly angry over paying too much for his home, shot the agent at point-blank range in the side of his head. The client had visited a second real estate agent after deciding to sell the home, but given the current climate in the real estate market, he was told the home was not worth what he had paid for it. The client apparently placed the blame squarely on the shoulders of his former real estate agent and took matters into his own hands." (www.woodtv.com)*

Most of the time, distraught clients are upset "in the moment" and their anger or frustration will diffuse before it becomes an issue. There are times, however when upset or angry clients may call or even come into your office. It is important that your receptionist, your first line of defense, is well versed and trained on how to deal with this situation. If the receptionist feels immediately threatened, every effort to call 911 should be made.

Whether in person or on the phone, the staff member should follow these guidelines.

- Remain calm.
- Try not to escalate the situation.

- Establish an escape route or vocalize personal limitations if on the phone.
- Involve witnesses or record the call if on the phone.
- Activate response plan. (If your company does not have a response plan, please contact us through www.justbesafe.com to develop one.)
- Give the person your full attention.
- Restate/validate their concerns.
- Ask for their suggestions on what your company can do to rectify the situation.
- Let them know what you can do.
- Follow through.

What Is Domestic Violence?

Domestic violence is a violent confrontation between family or household members involving physical harm, sexual assault, or fear of physical harm. Family or household members include spouses/former spouses, those in (or formerly in) a dating relationship, adults related by blood or marriage, and those who have a biological or legal parent-child relationship. Domestic violence destroys the home. No one deserves to be abused. The responsibility for the violence belongs to the abuser. It is not the victim's fault! (This information is provided by Steven Stewart, the prosecuting attorney for Clark County, Indiana, www.clarkprosecutor.org.)

Symptoms of Abuse

Any act used to gain power and control over another person is abuse. Look for the warning signs to recognize domestic abuse and keep in mind that there may be multiple warning signs occurring in your life or others around you. People who are abused physically are often isolated and their partners tend to control their lives as well as verbally degrade them.

Using Physical and Sexual Abuse

- Hair pulling
- Biting
- Shaking, pushing or pinching
- Choking or kicking
- Confinement
- Slapping, hitting or punching
- Using weapons
- Forced intercourse, unwanted sexual touching in public or in private
- Depriving food or sleep.

Using Emotional Abuse

- Insulting someone in public or in private
- Putting the person down in front of friends and family
- Making a person feel bad about themselves
- Calling them names
- Making a person think they are crazy
- Playing mind games
- Humiliating them

- Making them feel guilty
- Using male privilege and acting like "Master of the Castle"
- Treating them like a servant
- Making all the big decisions
- Being the one to define men and women's roles.

Using Economic Abuse

- Preventing them from getting or keeping a job
- Making them ask for money
- Giving them an allowance
- Taking their money
- Not letting them know about or have access to family income
- Not allowing them a voice in important financial decisions
- Demanding exclusive control over household finances.

Using Coercion and Threats

- Making or carrying out threats to do something to hurt them
- Threatening to leave, or to commit suicide
- Threatening to report them to welfare or child services

Using Intimidation

- Making them afraid by using looks, gestures, or actions
- Making them do illegal things

- Throwing or smashing things, destroying property
- Abusing pets
- Dangerous driving
- Displaying weapons.

Using Children

- Making them feel guilty about the children
- Using the children to relay messages
- Using visitation to harass them
- Threatening to take the children away.

Using Isolation

- Controlling what they do, who they see, what they read and where they go
- Limiting their outside involvement
- Refusing to let them learn to drive, go to school, or get a job
- Not allowing them to freely use the car or the telephone.

Using Jealousy And Blame To Justify Actions

- Minimizing, Denying, Blaming
- Making light of the abuse and not taking their concerns about it seriously
- Checking up on where they've been or who they've talked to
- Accusing them of infidelity
- Saying the abuse didn't happen
- Shifting responsibility for abusive behavior
- Saying they caused it

Why Get Help?

The danger is real.

Abuse is used to dominate, intimidate and manipulate. If you are controlling or have a controlling partner, don't ignore these behaviors. They are not the result of stress, anger, drugs or alcohol. They are learned behaviors that are destructive and dangerous. If the abuse continues without outside help, the abusing partner may risk being arrested, going to jail, or losing the relationship.

Domestic violence hurts all family members. When someone is abusive, she eventually loses the trust and respect of her partner. Abused partners are afraid to communicate their feelings and needs. Children witness the abuse and think the behavior is acceptable.

Everyone has the right to feel safe in a relationship. With help, people who are abusive can learn to be non-violent.

Learn the Warning Signs

In any relationship, disagreements develop. Domestic violence is not a disagreement, but a whole pattern of behaviors. In domestic violence one partner establishes and maintains power and control over their partner. These behaviors can become more frequent and intense over time.

Only the abusive person is responsible for these behaviors and only they can change them. Get help! Don't wait until you and the ones you love get hurt. You are not alone. You can talk with friends, a pastor or another trusted person about your situation. You can also seek help from victim assistance programs and domestic violence units in your city.

Threatening or Harassing Phone Calls/Text Messages

Regardless of the source, threatening phone calls or text messages are disturbing and should be taken seriously. Phone harassment is a general term used to describe any kind of unwanted telephone calls that's intended to cause upset, grief or alarm. Aside from invading your privacy, it is a form of bullying. The caller might know the victim, or may be dialing randomly. It may be a one-time call, or a string of abuse. Whatever the case, it's unacceptable in any shape or form, and has to be stopped. While threatening text messages are increasing and it is easier to block the number, there are still people out there who will figure out how to do it.

If you get a harassing call, you need to pay close attention to:

- Any background noise
- The caller's sex, accent and speech pattern
- Anything else that might aid in identification

Don't rely on your memory. Keep a log of any calls received, including date, time and details of each.

If calls are received on an answering machine or voicemail, save the information so it can be given to police.

Here are some additional tips:

- Hang up immediately if there is no response to your greeting.
- Hang up as soon as you hear anything inappropriate, like obscenity or an improper question.
- Do not conduct your own investigation or try to identify the caller. The caller wants to hear your voice. So, don't satisfy him by staying on the line.
- Anything you say can be misinterpreted and come out as encouragement, so do not give witty or sarcastic responses.
- The caller needs help in a clinical setting. Leave that to the professionals.
- Don't let the caller know that you are upset or angry.
- Be careful when the caller says she is taking a survey. If you have any concern about the legitimacy of the call, obtain the caller's name, business name and phone number. Say that you will call back after you verify the authenticity of the survey.
- Never give out personal information like your name or address to an unknown caller.
- Report harassing or obscene telephone calls to the police. Make a record of all crank calls. An

appropriate investigation will be made within the limits of investigative leads and technological capabilities.

Take extra precautions if you are being harassed. The caller may be a stalker or overprotective boy- or girlfriend. Always walk with a buddy and keep your doors and windows locked in your car and at home. This point is not meant to scare you, but increase your personal safety awareness. You don't need to be paranoid-just be cautious.

In the Event of an Attack

Even the best safety plans are not infallible. In the unfortunate event that you do find yourself under attack, there are some steps you can take to minimize your risk of serious injury, or worse.

Survivor's Instinct

You may have heard the expression "fight or flight," but I have a different term, which I call, "Survivor's Instinct" because what we are really talking about is your life. Here are steps that you can take to reduce the chances of physical harm to yourself:

⇒ Run and call 911 when you can.
⇒ Remove yourself from the dangerous situation to minimize your risk of injury or being incapacitated by an attacker. You're wearing

your cell phone, like I told you to, right? Good. You'll have it with you to call 911 when you're in a safer place.

⇒ Take a self-defense training class.
⇒ Developing your self-defense skills to the point that you react on instinct is the perfect way to avoid being frozen by panic if you are attacked. Criminals don't expect their victims to fight back, and many will flee if they encounter resistance.
⇒ If you strike, mean it. You know how hunters say that a wounded bear is more dangerous than a healthy one? The same goes for criminals. If you launch a counterstrike against a predator and don't incapacitate him long enough to get away, he'll get the impression that you're too weak to defend yourself and come back at you with a vengeance. He won't just be trying to frighten you the second time either; he'll be trying to seriously hurt you.

When faced with danger, trust yourself and stay as calm as possible. Think rationally and evaluate your options. This is easier said than done. Self-defense training can be a vital boost here. It will not only teach you how to respond to various types of attack, but also help train your thought processes so you can respond quickly and instinctively. S.A.F.E. offers these classes; visit www.justbesafe.com to sign up for one or request a class through your REALTORS® association.

Five Strategies for Response

There is no one right way to respond to a confrontation, because each situation is different. Your response should depend on the circumstances: the location of the attack, your personal resources, the characteristics of the assailant, and the presence of weapons. There are many strategies that are effective, but you must rely on your own judgment to choose the best one:

- **No resistance** - Not resisting may be the proper choice in a situation. An attacker with a gun or a knife may put you in a situation where you think it is safer to do what he says. If someone tries to rob you, give up your property – don't give up your life.
- **Stalling for time** - Appear to go along with the attacker. This may give you time to assess the situation. When his guard is down, try to escape.
- **Distraction and then flight** - Obviously you should try to get away, but whether you can escape depends on your shoes, your clothing, your physical stamina, the terrain, and how close your predator is to you.
- **Verbal assertiveness** - If someone is coming toward you, hold out your hands in front of you and yell, "Stop" or "Stay back!" When interviewed, rapists said they'd leave a woman alone if she yelled or showed that she was not afraid to fight back.
- **Physical resistance** - If you decide to respond physically, remember that your first priority is to

get away. Act quickly and decisively to throw the attacker off guard while you escape.

Make a conscious effort to get an accurate description of your attacker(s). Even the smallest details may give authorities a clue to finding the suspect. Law enforcement states that you should tell authorities everything that occurred and what was said during the incident, including the things that may seem unimportant.

What to Remember

- The number one key to self-defense is to breathe. When you are caught off guard, the first human reaction is to shrink within yourself and hold your breath. Letting the air out will give you the chance to use the greatest weapon you have, which is your brain.
- If there is nothing else that can be done, if you have decided you must stand and fight, use any thing and any means you can:
    - Heel of your shoe
    - Umbrella
    - Keys
    - Hair spray
    - Comb
    - Flashlight
    - Fireplace tool

- When faced with danger, trust yourself and stay as calm as possible. Well, let's be honest; that is not possible without breathing.

Think rationally and evaluate your options. Each confrontation is different. While a self-defense course can prepare you for many types of attack, the element of surprise will often throw you so much that you can't remember anything. But planning and practicing your actions ahead of time will help. Always remember that your priority is to get away and call 911. And don't forget to breathe!

Before You Put Them in Your Car

"Safety is something that happens between your ears, not something you hold in your hands."

Jeff Cooper

Five
Before You Put Them in Your Car

Driving with clients is one of the most dangerous traditions that real estate agents practice. The argument for doing this is valid; it gives you uninterrupted time with your prospective buyers, allowing you to ask questions that will help you better understand their needs and wants. I understand and agree; however, let me give you a scenario to consider.

A husband and wife meet you at your office and you invite them into your car. As you drive out of the parking lot, the husband or the wife pulls a gun on you and gives you new directions. What will you do now?

Obviously, you are in deep trouble with few options. I would like to tell you there are ways to get out of this situation. The movies and TV dramas lead us to believe you can jump out of a car at a stoplight or stop sign, and although bruised, you would not only survive but walk away from this scenario. Maybe that will work for you. You could slam your vehicle into an object like a tree or light pole, and hope the air bag deploys. That might work for you as well, but my experience from talking with survivors and criminals has taught me that better preparation would be the best defense.

My first question is why are they in your car at all? Even though you've made a big production out of qualifying your clients while still in the office, it's always a good idea to take separate cars to any properties you're showing them. You can use the excuse that you are expected somewhere else afterward and won't be returning to the office, if you wish. (This has the added advantage of letting them know that someone will be aware if you don't show up at this other place by a certain time.)

If putting them in your car is your only choice, then I recommend that you bring at least one other person beside yourself. (Remember in Chapter One what I told you your mother said about there being safety in numbers?) I also recommend that you have at least one pepper spray clipped to the driver's side door, and that your partner be texting or having a brief conversation telling someone where you are and that you will be back in touch within the hour. Criminals generally pick easy victims, which include agents working alone who put themselves in harm's way.

The Ten-Second Rule

This is one of the most overused terms in regards to real estate professionals' safety. It is also one of the best techniques that you can use. My issue with the Ten-Second Rule is that it is outdated. So let's first take a quick look at the Ten-Second Rule.

- Take 2 Seconds when you arrive at your destination.
- Take 2 Seconds after you step out of your car.
- Take 2 Seconds as you walk towards your destination.
- Take 2 Seconds at the door.
- Take 2 Seconds as soon as you enter your destination.

The problem is not with the Ten-Second Rule but with us. We are busy and always multitasking. When we arrive at our destination we all know we should stop and take a look around, but we don't. So instead of taking ten seconds, can you take one? Let's look at how we have scaled down the Ten-Second Rule to be the Five-Second Rule.

The Five-Second Rule

Take 1 Second when you arrive at your destination.

- Is there any questionable activity in the area?
- Are you parked in a well-lit, visible location?
- Can you be blocked in?

Take 1 Second after you step out of your car.

- Are there suspicious people around?
- Do you know exactly where you're going?

Take 1 Second as you walk towards your destination.

- Are people coming and going or is the area unusually quiet?
- Do you observe any obstacles or hiding places in the parking lot or along the street?
- Is anyone loitering in the area?

Take 1 Second at the door.

- Do you have an uneasy feeling as you're walking in?
- Is someone following you in?

Take 1 Second as soon as you enter your destination.

- Does anything seem out of place?
- Is anyone present who shouldn't be there or who isn't expected?

5 Seconds TOTAL

Taking in your surroundings lets you spot and avoid danger. Make it a habit. Then share it with someone else.

Again, remember **Andrew's Golden Rule of Safety**.

You are your best weapon, your voice, mind and body. Listen and trust your inner voice. It is the best weapon you have.

In addition to the five seconds you just took to secure your environment, there are a number of other tips you can take to stay safe that we will cover throughout this book. Remember that a criminal's goal is to isolate you and catch you off guard.

Don't forget to carry your cell phone with you at all times. Clip it on, or put it in your pocket, and make it part of your apparel. If you keep your cell phone in a purse or briefcase, or in the car, it may not be available when you need it most.

Carjacking

The first step to avoiding an attack is to stay alert at all times and be aware of your environment. The most likely places for a carjacking are:

- Stop signs and stop lights
- Parking lots
- Residential driveways

Let me ask you a question. How far behind the car in front of you should you be at a stoplight, legally? This was a question on your driver's license test but let me give you the correct answer. You should have one-half of your vehicle's length in front and behind you. (You should always be able to see the rear tires of the vehicle in front of you.) This would allow you to maneuver easily if necessary.

You don't want to be trapped anywhere. If you're the first car at the light, make sure you stop behind the line painted on the roadway. This not only trips the sensor to change the light to green for you in the next cycle, it also gives you an escape route.

In traffic, look around for possible avenues of escape. When stopped, use your rear and side view mirrors to stay aware of your surroundings. Also, keep your doors locked and windows up. This increases your safety and makes it more difficult for an attacker to surprise you.

Common Carjacking Scenarios

Accidents are one ruse used by attackers to control a victim. The following are common attack plans as reported by AAA Motor Club.

The Bump - The attacker bumps the victim's vehicle from behind. The victim gets out to assess the damage and exchange information. The victim's vehicle is taken.

Good Samaritan - The attacker(s) stages what appears to be an accident. They may simulate an injury. The victim stops to assist, and the vehicle is taken.

The Ruse - The vehicle behind the victim flashes its lights or the driver waves to get the victim's attention. The attacker tries to indicate that there is a problem with the victim's car. The victim pulls over and the vehicle is taken.

The Trap - Carjackers use surveillance to follow the victim home. When the victim pulls into his driveway and waits for the gate or garage door to open, the attacker pulls up behind and blocks the vehicle.

Parking Lot Safety

When you're going somewhere at night, you automatically think to park in a well-lit area. But what if it's still light outside when you park, but will be dark when you return to your vehicle? Keep this in mind when choosing a parking space. Whether in your office lot, a shopping center, or a condominium you're showing, parking lots are full of opportunities for criminals.

Most of us have a remote-entry system for our cars these days, so you're not spending time fumbling with your keys to unlock the door when you reach your vehicle. However, staying safe in any parking lot starts long before you ever emerge from your car or even arrive there.

When you pull into a lot, find a space that's not only going to be well lit after dark, but isn't close to a wall or shrubbery that could provide a hiding place for an attacker. If there's a vehicle that has tinted windows so that you cannot see into the vehicle, don't park near it. Criminals have often used such vehicles to grab unsuspecting victims and take them somewhere else.

Another thing to watch for when choosing your parking space is dead-ends. Could someone park behind you and prevent you from driving away? If you're parking at a single-family home, try to park on the street so another car can't block you into the driveway.

Parking lot criminals use the same strategies with ATMs. Criminals have been known to pull cars in front of and behind the lane so the victim could not escape. Watch for such traps and avoid situations that could put you in danger.

If you have anything with you, valuable or not, secure it in your trunk before arriving at your destination. Criminals who are casing a parking lot watch for people locking items in their trunks, and know that if they break a window there's a button they can push inside the car that will release the trunk. Some vehicles have back seats that fold down exposing the trunk or hatchback.

Never leave anything in sight in your car, as thieves will quickly break a window to get at anything that looks to be of value. Your old stereo may be destined for the recycling center, but if it looks like something a thief could easily fence, it could make your vehicle a target. Keep it out of sight.

When arriving at your destination, before you turn off your car while your seat belt is still fastened, with your windows rolled up, and your air conditioning still running, take five seconds and look around.

Is there a van parked next to you? If so, move to another parking space.

What is close to you that will serve as a landmark? Are there people standing around?

What does that little voice inside you say?

Walking to and from Your Vehicle

Before exiting your vehicle, take a few seconds to look around you and make sure there aren't any suspicious people or vehicles nearby. Then make sure you know exactly where you're going once you get out. Keep your doors locked until the moment you're ready to exit.

Gather all the things that you are taking with you while sitting in your front seat. We have all seen the backside of someone getting things out of their back seat. I wish they knew how vulnerable they are in that situation. If you cannot gather your things from the front seat, open the back door, sit in your back seat and get your things together.

Be alert and very aware of your surroundings if you're retrieving something from your trunk; you are extremely vulnerable to an attacker at that time. Don't bend over and dig endlessly inside the trunk. Remain aware and alert.

As you are walking away from your vehicle, take a few seconds. Turn around and use your remote to again lock your car. (This usually sets the car's alarm, and also gives the perception that you are paying attention to your surroundings.)

Once your doors are locked and you're walking to your destination, remain aware of what is going on around you. If you are carrying a purse, carry it on the side facing away from passing traffic to keep someone from driving by and grabbing it off your shoulder. Steer clear of anyone loitering in the area, and be wary of anyone approaching you quickly.

When walking back to your car in the parking lot, turn around as you leave and look at the building where you just exited. Look like, "did I forget something?" This turn is crucial because it gives the perception that you are paying attention to your surroundings and sends the message that the element of surprise will not be available to anyone with bad intentions.

<u>While there's no need for paranoia, a healthy dose of awareness is important to maintain</u>. If you're daydreaming, looking at the ground or chatting on the phone as you walk through a parking lot, it's a clear sign to a criminal that you're not paying attention to your surroundings and may make a good victim.

As you return to your vehicle, remain aware of what's going on around you. Get your keys out before you leave the building, and keep your hand on your remote (does yours have a panic button?) If your current vehicle does not have a remote unlocking system, you should definitely consider it for your next one.

If you have pepper spray, keep it in your hand as well. Use your remote to unlock the door as you're approaching it so the time you spend outside the vehicle is minimal.

Don't unlock or open the actual car door until you're ready to enter the vehicle. If you have the option of opening only the driver's door, do that unless there are others riding with you.

If you have packages, signs, or other items to put in the trunk, glance around before opening it, and remain alert as you're placing the items inside.

All of this is especially true if you're with a child; criminals know that mothers are most concerned about the safety of their children. They also know that children can be very distracting and will use that to gain an advantage. While you wouldn't usually have your child with you while showing a property, you may if you're placing signs or stopping into the office to pick up something. Don't let a sense of urgency prevent you from being cautious.

Once inside the vehicle, immediately lock the doors. Real estate agents are known for spending a few minutes sitting in their car once they get in. They have to organize whatever they were carrying, check phone messages, program the GPS and any number of other things that make them completely unaware of anything going on around them. It's the perfect time for a criminal to jump into the passenger side of the car, or snatch the driver's side door open and stick a gun to the agent's head. If that doesn't sound appealing to you, make sure it doesn't happen by locking your doors and getting underway as quickly as possible.

It is crucial to pay attention to your surroundings. Just a few seconds of looking around, but more importantly paying attention to yourself and your behavior is the most important thing you can do.

Remember Andrew's Golden Rule of Safety:

You are your best weapon, your mind, voice, and body. Listen and trust your inner voice. It is the best weapon you have.

Safety while Driving

Most of us took driver's education back in high school. We learned about safe driving tactics that would keep us from getting into accidents.

What about techniques that can keep us from becoming victims of crime?

The awareness you had of your surroundings when you were walking to your vehicle should remain with you as you're behind the wheel. You may remember being told in driver's education to check your rearview mirror every so often. This can also be a deterrent to attack. News reports of "bumper rapists" circulate from time to time, and ramming into their intended victims is a method used by some criminals to get you out of your car.

While you may not be able to avoid being hit by someone who intentionally hits you, knowing it is coming will give you a moment to consider your response.

You and I both know that you'll be talking on the phone when you're in the car, so I won't even tell you not to do that. Not only is it against the law in some states, but you would be more aware of your surroundings if you were not talking on the phone. If you must, then consider using a hands-free device, whether a Bluetooth headset, a built-in phone in the car or similar hands-free solutions.

This keeps both your hands free to handle whatever unexpected traffic situation may arise. As you approach a red light, watch out for people begging for money on the side of the road. We all know that there are people who are truly homeless or less fortunate than ourselves, but trust me, they are rarely the people you see holding a sign at intersections.

Some of these people make more money from begging than we make working! What's more, many of them have criminal intentions toward unsuspecting motorists who take pity on them and leave themselves vulnerable. If you must give one of these people money, stop your car about ten to fifteen feet before you get to them, put your window down and toss the money out of the window.

Then put your window back up, make sure your door is locked, and continue to pull up to the light. The beggar will go over there to pick up the money, and you won't be putting yourself in danger of being knifed, pepper sprayed or shot through your open window.

These same people who beg for money at intersections are also on the lookout for items they can easily fence to buy drugs or booze. GPS systems make an ideal target; so don't put yourself in the crosshairs by leaving yours out if you're not using it at the moment. It will also minimize the time you spend putting things away and getting situated when you reach your destination.

Mishaps on the Road

No one is immune from occasional mishaps while on the road. Sure we know we're supposed to keep our cars in good working order, but we're busy. We all neglect things from time to time. We forget to check the oil or tire pressure or miss a scheduled maintenance visit. And sometimes, things just happen. The radiator bursts or a tire goes flat. But, much more than a mere inconvenience, these incidents can also place our personal safety in jeopardy.

When something does go wrong, there are some steps you can take to minimize your risk. One of those is to prepare ahead of time for potential mishaps.

When it comes to commuting or traveling any lengthy distance, a roadside emergency kit can mean the difference between getting back on the road and being stuck for a long period of time. All kits contain the same basic items but don't forget to customize it with things you may need personally. For instance, most professionals wear dress shoes daily so you may want to have a pair of tennis shoes in your kit in case you need to walk a long distance. You may also want to include a jacket and rain gear in case of bad weather.

Some of the basic items include:

- △ 12-foot jumper cables
- △ Four 15-minute roadside flares
- △ Two quarts of oil
- △ Gallon of antifreeze
- △ First aid kit (including an assortment of bandages, gauze, adhesive tape, antiseptic cream, instant ice and heat compresses, scissors and aspirin)
- △ Blanket
- △ Extra fuses
- △ Flashlight and extra batteries
- △ Tools - Flat head and Phillips screwdrivers, pliers, vise grips, adjustable wrench
- △ Tire inflator (such as a Fix-A-Flat)
- △ Tire pressure gauge
- △ Rags
- △ Roll of paper towels
- △ Roll of duct tape
- △ Spray bottle with washer fluid
- △ Pocketknife

- Ice scraper
- Pen and paper
- Help sign
- Granola or energy bars
- Bottled water

If you have an accident, breakdown or get a flat tire, you may find yourself stuck on the side of the road for a long time. If you do not have a roadside assistance plan of some type, I recommend you get one. Road service clubs like AAA, some cellular service providers, insurance companies and automobile manufactures (OnStar, TeleAid, COMMAND) offer roadside assistance.

Once you call for help, you'll still be waiting before it arrives. Here are some tips to keep you safe while you wait.

- If your engine is working, keep it running and run the air conditioning (or heat, depending on the weather). If the engine is disabled, roll down the windows, but stay in the car.
- Keep doors locked.
- Keep an eye on your belongings and your car if you must get out.
- Keep your keys and pepper spray in your hand if you must leave the car.
- If you have been in an accident, do not leave the scene before the police arrive. If the other driver tries to leave, get the license plate number and description of the driver and car to give to police when they arrive.

- Call someone to let them know where you are and have them meet you there.
- Inform your office and buddy.

Prepare for the worst. If it doesn't happen, there is no harm done. But if it does, you'll be glad you thought ahead. (www.AAA.com and www.edmunds.com)

Ten Quick Reminders

1. Always have your keys out and ready before leaving a building to approach your vehicle. Searching through a purse or briefcase after you've reached your car provides criminals an excellent opportunity to sneak up on you.
2. Be especially alert when leaving stores or shopping malls for your vehicle. This is a time when criminals know you are carrying cash, checkbooks, credit cards, or other valuables.
3. Look around and inside your vehicle before you get in. If you are concerned for any reason, simply walk past your car and call for help.
4. Lock your door immediately upon entering the vehicle. Make this your first action—even before you put the key in the ignition. Lock your door every time you get into your car—even if you are going for only a short ride.
5. Check your surroundings before getting out of your car. If something or someone strikes you as out of place or threatening, drive away. If it's dark, go to a well lit, heavily traveled area.

6. Use a two-piece key ring with your car keys separate from your other important keys. Give parking valets or mechanics your car keys only. Supplying the entire set of keys creates an opportunity for duplicates to be made.
7. Avoid stairwells in parking garages. Try walking down the auto ramp instead. As long as you watch for cars, the ramp can be much safer.
8. I have to say it: Avoid talking on your cell phone while you drive. Concentrate on your driving, not your conversation. If you have to make a call, pull over to the side of the road. If you're making a call using your cell phone, never discuss important information such as travel plans or credit card numbers. For less than $100, anyone can buy scanning equipment and listen in on your cellular phone conversations.
9. If you are involved in an accident, remain in your vehicle if at all possible. Immediately call for help and wait for assistance.

10. Maintain your vehicle in good working condition. If a breakdown occurs, remember your safety comes first.

What Would You Do?

In each of these scenarios, choose the best answer from among those provided. You'll find the safest solutions provided in Appendix Four.

Scenario 1

You are walking to your car from the office after dark, regretting that the only parking place earlier in the day had been near some bushes at the far end of the lot. Suddenly, a feeling comes over you that something is not right. Glancing around, you don't see anything out of the ordinary, and there appears to be no one else around. As you approach your car, a man springs out of the bushes, shows what appears to be a knife, and screams, "Gimme the purse!" What would you do?

a. Wet your pants.
b. Put your hands out in front of you and yell, "Stop!"
c. Throw your purse as far away from your car as you can, and when he runs to get it, quickly unlock your car, get in and immediately lock the doors and call 911.
d. Toss your purse to him, while backing away and you should have been talking to someone on the phone as you were walking. (Remember what Andrew said.)

Scenario 2

On your way into the office at six-thirty in the morning, you stop by to pick up some donuts for your clients who are coming in to sign some papers on their way to work. As you walk back across the parking lot to your car, you can see that in the few minutes you were away, someone has smashed a window and stolen your GPS system. What would you do?

a. Call your clients and tell them you'll be a little late.
b. Go back into the donut shop, where there are other people, and call 911 on your cell phone.
c. Curse at yourself for not putting the GPS system into the glove box, like Andrew told you to do.
d. Look around to see if the thief is still in sight and chase after him as you call 911 on your cell phone.

Open Houses and Listing Appointments

"Working safely may get old, but so do those who practice it."

Unknown Author

Six
Open Houses and Listing Appointments

Open Houses

The problem that I see with safety at open houses is simply a lack of preparation. Remember when you started in the business and you used to preview the house, check out the neighborhood, talk with other agents about the neighborhood, visit the community and do your research?

Now what happens? The morning of the open house you toss some signs in the trunk of your car, stop by the grocery store and pick up some snacks, drop off some signs close to the home and go into the home you are showing to wait for people to show up.

It is lack of preparedness that increases your chances of victimization. So, when I ask the question, "Is having an open house a good idea?" I answer yes.

When posed to a group of real estate agents, this question can be counted on to trigger animated debate. For every agent or broker who believes that an open house is an effective way to market a home and generate leads, there is another who believes it is a complete waste of time. Regardless of which side you're on, in order to do an open house safely, you must remember the three Ps.

Preparedness Preparedness Preparedness

Be prepared for specific or unpredictable events or situations. You can start with these common safety tips for hosting an open house.

- Don't advertise a listing as vacant.
- Establish escape routes from each level of the house.
- Call the office or a buddy hourly.
- Keep your keys and cell phone with you.
- Park where you can get out quickly.
- Make sure all deadbolt locks are unlocked to facilitate a faster escape.
- Double check the backyard to make sure you can get past any fence if necessary.
- When leaving the property, secure the house and check all windows and doors.
- When showing the property, avoid attics, basements and getting trapped in small rooms; let prospects lead the way into rooms.
- Notify neighbors in advance or, if time permits, introduce yourself to the neighbors and let them know when you will be showing a house. They will be more alert to unusual sounds and you will have somewhere to run to if you need help.
- Remind sellers to put valuables in a safe, secure place. Do not leave your briefcase, purse or laptop sitting on a counter.

- Be aware of suspicious behavior and your surroundings.
- When prospects begin arriving at the open house, jot down their car description, license number and a physical description of each person. This will assist you in remembering names as well.
- Note items of interest in several areas of the home, so you can use them as distractions if needed. You may want to keep a supply of 3x5" cards handy to jot down features by room.
- Have a prearranged distress code.

While all these tips are good, how practical are they? How many do you practice? How often do you complete all of them? Based upon thousands of conversations with agents that conduct open houses, law enforcement agencies, and medical practitioners, we have developed a system that can dramatically decrease the chances you will become a victim.

When you're showing a home, whether it's an open house or in a private showing, your primary focus is on selling it, right? Sure, but don't let that keep you from being aware of your safety. But how do you know where safety lies in an unfamiliar neighborhood?

Simple – you preview the property and the neighborhood. Previewing any property you're selling is a secret shared by the best in the real estate business. Here's how it's done, from the perspective of safety.

In the days before you meet the client, visit the property. This will enable you to speak intelligently about the area, giving clients the lowdown on features like school bus stops, yoga in the park, and the location of the closest grocery store. It also gives you an opportunity to put several pieces of your safety plan into place.

Walk the surrounding neighborhood, if possible. You will learn much more about it than if you drove. If any of the neighbors are out, introduce yourself and let them know you'll be showing the house. Identify your car for them, so they'll know it's you. Go up to the doors of the houses on either side and across the street from the property you're showing to meet those neighbors. For an open house, offer them the opportunity to tour the home half an hour before it's open to the public. This has four benefits to you:

- Neighbors are all curious about the house that's for sale. They want to see it, learn the asking price and compare it to the value of their own home. They may have a friend who wants to move into the neighborhood or they may need an agent to sell their own home someday. So, it gets qualified buyers into the house.
- Second, it may be creating future business for you. We all know that familiarity builds trust.
- Third, these neighbors may reveal things about the neighborhood you hadn't noticed yourself. This can give you additional selling features to highlight to your clients.
- Fourth, and most importantly, it familiarizes those people with you and makes them aware you'll be there.

While you're in the neighborhood, visit the local police substation to let them know you'll be at the property, and during what hours. If you're hosting an open house, tell them you'll have refreshments for any officers who stop by. Do the same at the local fire station. That way, there are two groups of emergency responders who will know you'll be in the house, and when. What's more, you've extended the invitation for them stop by.

Make at least three trips to preview the property. Yes, it's time-consuming, but it will also give you an excellent overview of the property and surrounding streets. Not only will you really impress your clients, you'll know just what to do if something goes wrong.

Before the Open House

On the day of the open house or showing – first thing in the morning:

- Locate the lockbox.
- Determine where you and your clients will park.

- Find out if there are any pets of which you need to beware.

- Does the property have a privacy fence? If so, is there a gate? Where does it lead?
- Look at the shrubs – do they provide a hiding place for someone?
- Make a mental note of where the garage door is.
- Also note any other unique features of the house.

- Find some interesting feature that's not near the front door.

At your appointment time:

- Note what's going on in the neighborhood at that time of day.
- Notice who's around. Are there many people? This is a great time to introduce yourself.
- Check again for pets.
- Make note of whether you have cell phone reception in the neighborhood and inside the property.
- Is anyone else having an open house? If you have the opportunity to introduce yourself to the agent in charge of it, do so.

Open House at Night:

- Note any outside lighting around the house, including streetlights.
- Note any areas where landscaping may provide hiding places.
- Make any adjustments to your parking location, as dictated by the two factors above.

There are many other aspects to safely showing a home to clients. Doing your homework by previewing the property is only the first step to ensuring your safety. So now, you're in on the secret!

And remember Andrew's Golden Rule of Safety

"You are your best weapon, your mind, voice, and body. Listen and trust your inner voice. It is the best weapon you have."

A Review of the Ol' Preview Trick

1. Visit the property and neighborhood a few days before the open house. Ideally, visit at least three times, at different times of day and in the evening. If anyone else is having an open house at the same time, introduce yourself and let them know about yours.
2. Walk the neighborhood, introducing yourself to the neighbors and familiarizing them with your vehicle. For an open house, offer them the opportunity to tour the home half an hour before it's open to the public.
3. Visit the nearest police substation and fire station to let them know you'll be showing the house, and during what hours. Tell them you'll have refreshments for any officers who stop by. Not only do these two groups of emergency responders know you're in the neighborhood, you've extended the invitation for them stop by. And because you don't know exactly when they will, neither will the criminals.
4. A nighttime visit is especially important when you're hosting an open house. Note the property's lighting, landscaping issues, and parking situation at that time.

5. Note items of interest in several areas of the home, so you can use them as distractions if needed. You may want to keep a supply of 3x5" cards handy to jot down features by room.

During the Open House

Having prepared ahead of time, you'll be much more confident on the day of your open house.

You'll need to arrive at the property at least an hour early on the day of the open house to get set up and make sure everything is in order. Set up your sign-in sheet on the desk. If feasible, you should set up your desk in the garage so that you are in plain view to passersby and neighbors. Turn on the lights throughout the house. Locate all the exit doors so you can find them quickly if you need to escape.

Place decorative bells on each exit door handle so you'll be able to hear if someone goes in or out of them. If you haven't already prepared your 3x5" cards with interesting features, this is a perfect time to do so. Unlock any deadbolts so you won't have to fumble with keys if you need to escape from an attacker.

If you've promised to show the home to the neighbors early, make sure you're ready for them.

You'll spend a fair amount of your time sitting at the desk you've set up in the garage. As prospects walk in, stand to greet them, and then ask them to jot down their information on the sign-in sheet. While they're doing that, evaluate them. Do you feel comfortable with them? Is there anything remotely suspicious about them?

If you're at all uneasy, pick up the phone and call "John," or whatever name you want to use. Tell your imaginary friend that you've just had someone stop in and you won't be able to come there to meet him, and ask if he can come there to visit you instead. Pause as though he's replying and then say something like, "Okay; I'll see you in a few minutes." This gives the prospects the impression that someone else's arrival is imminent, and if they'd planned anything unsavory, perhaps they'd better move on to another house.

We've all worked open houses where we sit there bored for hours, then all of a sudden, a busload of people show up at once. When this happens, there's no way for you to keep track of all these people at once. This is where your 3x5" cards come in handy. You can be standing with one couple and say, "Take a look at the (whatever feature off your card) in the (room). I'll be right there to answer any questions for you." This lets people know you're keeping tabs on them and makes them think you're coming their way. You can do all of this politely if you remember Andrew's Acronym, – "KWK – Kill'em with Kindness."

Closing Up

As the time draws near for your open house to end, be especially aware of your surroundings. A criminal would see this as a perfect opportunity to catch you off guard as you're packing up and preparing to leave.

This is a great time for your buddy to join you. That could be someone from your office, a family member, or even a real estate professional from down the street.

If it's another agent, secure one house, then you can go to the other and secure it together.

There is also an order of closing up that will help you stay safe.

1. Walk through each room to make sure nobody else is left in the home. If you find someone, let them know you're closing and ask them to meet you out front. While you are out front waiting on any lingering guests, load your vehicle with the open house signs, and any other items you brought in the house.
2. Secure the entry door used by most guests. If you've set up your desk in the garage, shut the garage door.
3. Then work from the back of the house to the front, securing each external entry door and collecting your decorative bells placed there earlier.
4. As you go through the house, make sure all the windows are closed and locked. Check all the closets to make sure they're empty and someone hasn't decided to hide in one until you're gone. Turn off the lights as you go, working your way to your point of exit.
5. Check the outside surroundings through a front window before you exit the house and lock the front door behind you as you leave.

6. Be aware of your surroundings as you enter your vehicle to drive away.

Extras

If someone from the police or fire department stopped by, you might want to stop by the substation on your way out of the neighborhood to thank them.

If the next-door neighbors stopped in, it would be good to let them know you've closed up and how much you appreciated them stopping by.

Be sure to advise your clients to remove or lock away documents that contain personal information that could be lifted and used to steal their identity.

Safety at Showing a Vacant Property

Let's have an honest conversation about showing vacant properties. Here's the conversation I've heard about:

> Client: "I saw a home on 123 Maple Street. I am interested in looking at it."
>
> Agent: "Great. Are you working with anyone? When do you want to see it?"
>
> Client: "Tonight at 6:30."

Agent: "I'll meet you there. Let me get your name and phone number in case something comes up."

You then gather information on the property, get information on similar properties, practice your pitch, grab a buyer's agreement, etc. Then you go meet the potential buyer at the property. Is this your process for showing appointments???

Here is what I would like you to do.

Meet the client in your office. Your broker and I asked you over and over again, but we know you. We know you won't do this. So, please take someone with you and never, never, ever go alone. Do you know these people? Do you know how many folks are going to be waiting for you when you arrive on this appointment? Use your buddy list. Is the potential commission worth your life? Let's look at this dialogue again.

Client: "I saw a home on 123 Maple Street that I am interested in looking at it."

Agent: "Great. Are you working with another agent? No? Good. When did you want to set up an appointment? We can meet somewhere close to the property and then go from there. Is tomorrow too soon for you?"

Client: "I was hoping to look at it this evening. Can't you just meet me there at the house?" (Are the alarms going off? They should be!)

Agent: "We have a safety process in our office. We never meet clients at the property. How about we meet at [name public location] at 5:30 or 6:00? It's about two blocks from the property. Let me get your name and phone number. Will you be coming from work or home?"

Client: "My name is John Doe, and my number is 555-1212. I'll be driving there immediately after work. I work downtown. It should take me about 20 minutes to get to [public location]."

Agent: "That seems about right. Where do you work John?"

Client: "I work at XXX Corporation."

Agent: "Great. I'll see you at [public location] at about 5:30 then."

This is what we learned about this client in that brief conversation:

- Serious buyers understand safety and want to work with professionals.
- You've gotten their name, their phone number, and their employer's name, which you will immediately research for validity.

You are better off losing a potential client then potentially losing your life. This isn't drama, it's life. Real estate agents have daily, one-on-one contact with virtual strangers and make themselves relatively easy targets for criminals. The National Association of REALTORS® reports an increase in crimes against real estate agents in recent years. Crimes range from minor thefts to assaults, rapes and even murder.

Qualifying the Prospect

Review the sections "The Rule of Five" and "Before You Put Them in Your Car" on what you need to do before leaving the office to qualify a prospect to whom you're about to show a property. Have you done these things? Here's a quick checklist to review.

1. Meet him in the office or a public location, like a restaurant.
2. Verify his identity.
3. Get his car make, model and license number.
4. Photocopy his driver's license.
5. Complete the Prospect Identification Form.

Yes, it takes a few minutes to do this, but how much time is your life worth? Don't get caught up in the excitement of a potential sale and forget these basic safety steps.

The Saturday Afternoon Phone Call

Saturday afternoon, you receive a phone call from a woman who states that she and her husband are at one of your properties, and would love to see it. Are you going to ask the client to wait until Monday and meet you at the office? No!

Are you going to ask the client to drive from the house and meet you at the office now? No, you are not, even though both your broker and I beg you to meet the client at the office! Since you are not going to do as we requested, let's give you some win-win tools to increase your safety.

Let the client know that you would love to show them the property. Tell the client that your office safety policy is to meet at a public location. Pick a location a few blocks from the property, like a Starbucks, Panera Bread, Burger King, or McDonalds, to meet. Tell your client to meet you there and you will buy them a cup of coffee.

Your Word Track

Here is the perfect word track to say when your prospects walk in the door. "Hello Mr. and Mrs. Smith. I look forward to showing you your new home, and I appreciate you meeting me here. My broker is a stickler for safety." By being upfront, you relieve any tension that may be present and honest people will appreciate that.

"I called my office and asked my assistant to research some additional homes in the area so I will have that information today." Again, what is safety? Safety is a perception. What you are doing is telling the client that someone knows where you are.

"Before we leave, our office policy requires that I see your driver's license. It's become a pretty standard practice these days." This assures the client that they are getting the same treatment that everyone else gets. Since you're not at your office, write down their pertinent information. Even better would be to have them complete an identification form with their phone number and employer information.

Folks, if people are reluctant to share their driver's license information with you that is the first red flag, A SERIOUS WARNING SIGN.

When they hand their driver's license to you, now it is time to use your wonderful cell phone to call your office, voicemail or answering service.

Your conversation should go like this: "Hello, this is Andrew and I am with Mr. and Mrs. Smith. Mr. Smith's driver's license number is 12345678. We are going to see the house at 1234 West Adams Lane. We should be there in about six minutes. Oh, there is a possibility of another home in the area that meets their qualifications, as well. OK, you check on it and I will call you back once we get to the home. Thanks."

Hand Mr. Smith back his driver's license and say, "All right, are you ready to see your new home? Why don't you follow me over there?"

Analysis

Now let's talk a minute about what you have just done.

- You have given the perception that you are a professional working as part of a team, and that your office is working on additional properties.
- You have given the perception that someone knows who you are with, their information, where you are going and when you will call back.

Preparing for the Journey

At this time you give them your business card with your cell number. Let them know what type of vehicle you are driving. Inform them that you will park on the street and they can pull into their new driveway. What you are really doing is removing the client from the front door so you never have to have your back turned on your client.

If you have the capability, you can Google the information they provided on their client form before you reach the house.

Now, what your clients do not know is that before you met them you went to the house, walked around the exterior, located the lockbox, opened it, removed the key, and checked out the interior of the home. The last thing you want to happen is to show up to a property and have seven to ten criminals waiting inside the home. You also noted at least one interesting feature that is visible when approaching the front door of the home. This might be a rose garden on the right side of the home or some unique shrubs on the left side of the home. Some agents even buy an expensive decorative yard piece that they take from home to home.

Plan Your Escape Routes

If you previewed the home, always familiarize yourself with all the possible escape routes. Imagine what you would do if you were being attacked while showing that home. Thinking through various scenarios helps you be mentally prepared in the event that the unthinkable does happen.

Use the home's unique features to your advantage.

By way of review, when you pull up and park in front of the house and your client parks in the driveway, as you walk up the driveway, the walkway narrows for only one person and the client suggests that you lead the way, you remark, "Hey, take a look at that… [Insert unique feature you noted earlier]."

While they are walking over to look, that's when you unlock and open the front door. By the time they have returned to you, you've turned to face them again. You have pulled your cell phone and are telling your office that you are at the home, and will check back on the additional properties in fifteen minutes.

Now you can devote your full attention to the remainder of the showing.

Politeness pays off.

Please remember: always let your clients lead the way. Do not lead the way yourself. It is too easy to be cornered or trapped in a room, basement or attic. Have your client go ahead of you. You can comment on each room from the safety of the door, from where you can flee more easily if you get a bad feeling about the situation.

All of these are actions you can take that will not make your clients think you are suspicious of them. You come across as polite, competent, and professional. It's all in the way you present things to them; be friendly and matter-of-fact about what you're doing, and they will be left with a positive impression of you.

Listing Appointments

Client: Hi, I have a home I need to sell. I heard you were a good Realtor to use. Can you meet me at my home tonight at 6:30 so we can discuss the details?

What do you do now?

I know we get excited about the possibility of a new listing and big sale. However we cannot let that excitement blur the lines of safety. Here are some tips that will keep you safe when getting a new listing.

1. **Identify sellers**. Check county property records, utilities, etc., to confirm the ownership of property before you go to a listing appointment or approach a FSBO. The more information you have, the easier and quicker it is for police to catch a perpetrator if you become a crime victim.
2. **Never go to a listing appointment alone.** Use the buddy system and take someone with you.
3. **Plan for success.** Know the sales area. Preview the property.
4. **Don't get greedy.** It's better to walk away from a listing or not show a house if you have an uneasy feeling. Trust your instincts!
5. **Phone home.** Let your office know where you are at all times. Arrange to call your office at a specific time and do it. No excuses.

What Would You Do?

In each of these scenarios, choose the best answer from among those provided. You'll find the safest solutions provided in Appendix Four.

Scenario 1

You've been working with a client for a few months and he just can't seem to find the right house, although you've shown him several that meet the needs he described to you. He calls you one day and wants to meet you at a house in a new development on the outskirts of town. He even gives you the directions to get there and seems very interested in this house. He wants to see it as soon as possible. You make an appointment with him for later in the afternoon, and then head over there to preview the house.

You have some trouble finding it, as the development is so new your GPS unit doesn't seem to have those streets on it yet and the directions he gave you seem to lead nowhere.

This development is so far out in the woods, you can't even get much of a signal on your cell phone. As you're driving through the development looking for the house, you notice a car just like your client's parked around the corner from where you finally locate the house. What would you do?

a. Park in the driveway of the house and start looking for a unique feature to mention to your client.
b. Park on the street in front of the house, call your buddy to give your location, and begin your preview activities.
c. Call someone on your buddy list and have them meet you. Don't meet the client until your buddy arrives.
d. Leave the area immediately and call your client to say that something's come up and you won't be able to show him the house this afternoon. Reschedule the appointment for another day.

Scenario 2

When you arrive to preview a house in a very upscale neighborhood, you find a dense privacy hedge planted across the front of the property so that the entrance to the house is not visible from the street.

The driveway goes past the side of the house, passing under a large porte-cochere by the side door on the way to the garage in the rear. Several mature trees and lush flower beds grace the front yard, while the back yard is filled with pathways, vine-laden arbors, and even a carp pond.

You notice more thick hedges planted near the front door that make it a very narrow entrance for a house of this size. When you return with your clients, how will you safely unlock the front door of the house without leaving yourself vulnerable to attack?

a. Ask the clients to wait in the car until you can get the front door open for them.
b. Direct clients to have a look at the porte-cochere, and while they are doing so, you unlock the front door.
c. Make note of the landscaping in the front yard and ask the clients to take a closer look at it; while they are doing so, you unlock the front door.
d. Hand the clients the key and have them unlock the front door while you wait behind them.

Scenario 3

A prospect who says they were referred to you by one of your Chamber of Commerce contacts calls on a Saturday morning and asks you about a house she's just spotted, and she wants to see it immediately.

Remembering your safety training, you ask her to meet you at a nearby Starbucks. She explains that she's going through a divorce and needs to find a house quickly.

But when you ask to see her driver's license, she gets nervous and says she'd left it at home when she changed purses that morning. What would you do?

a. Tell her you're sorry, but your broker insists that you can't show a house to anyone without a photo ID. Make an appointment for her to stop by the office on Monday, when you can get the proper paperwork completed to show her the house.

b. Never show an empty home alone, always take a buddy.

c. Call your buddy. Pretend that you're talking to your broker and discuss, in the client's earshot, how he's going to meet you at the house in fifteen minutes. Then agree to head over to the house with the client, with the understanding that your broker (actually, your buddy) will be arriving soon.

d. Have the prospect complete a Prospect Identification Form, then call your buddy to relay the information while you're sitting at Starbucks, so the client can hear you. Wait a few minutes for a call back to confirm that the information is valid, watching to see if the prospect backs down from seeing the house now, just in case the information she gave you is phony.

Scenario 4

You've been working an open house all afternoon and it's getting late in the day. You think everyone has left, but as you're making the rounds to lock up, you find a man who had come by earlier during a rush of people. You'd thought he'd left with them, but he's been lurking in one of the upstairs rooms. He pulls out a gun and tells you he's glad to catch you alone. What would you do?

a. Tell him your broker is due to stop by any minute.

b. Look around for something you can use to counterattack him.
c. Ask him what he wants, and make your choice to fight back or not fight back, either option is right as long as you are making the decision.
d. Put your hands out in front of you and yell, “Stop!”

The Number One Crime in the World

"Cleaning up after identity theft is a marathon, not a sprint. Prepare your mind accordingly."

Frank Mellott

Seven
The Number One Crime in the World

Document Security: Keeping Your Customers' Information Safe

The Gramm-Leach-Bliley (GLB) Act requires companies defined under the law as "financial institutions" to ensure the security and confidentiality of all their clients' information. The definition of "financial institution" under the Act is broad, and includes many businesses that may not normally describe themselves that way. Financial Institutions include any company that collects personal information from their customers or employees.

As part of its implementation of the GLB Act, the Federal Trade Commission (FTC) issued the Safeguards Rule, which requires financial institutions to have measures in place to keep customer information secure.

The Safeguards Rule applies to all businesses, regardless of size, that are "significantly engaged" in providing financial products or services. Many real estate offices collect personal information from their customers, including names, addresses, and phone numbers; bank and credit card account numbers; income and credit histories; and Social Security numbers.

It's the Law

If you dispose of your clients' valuable personal information carelessly you can be charged with a crime. In addition, there is a growing list of regulations that address information security, privacy and document retention that must be understood by businesses. Every business should have a shredder and use it on all documents containing personal information.

Non-compliance can result in serious legal problems from violations of the GLB Act and FACTA, the Fair and Accurate Credit Transactions Act, which requires anyone retaining consumer information for business purposes to destroy the personal information before discarding it.

Who Must Comply

These laws affect virtually all businesses. Your business is held responsible for protecting information if:

- You employ one or more people
- Your business keeps personal information on file for customers or employees
- Your business accepts credit cards for payment
- You buy or sell products on the Internet
- You do a credit check on an employee or potential customer

Background Checks

Does your company really trust its cleaning service? Have you ever left a customer sitting at your desk while you grabbed something in the other room? Did you leave documents from another customer in plain view? If you have an alarmed security system in place, do you change the code when employees or contractors are released? Are office keys stamped so they cannot be duplicated? Are client files kept in a secured location in locked files? These questions should all be addressed as part of your office security policy.

Identity Theft: What Your Customers Can Do

Your customers are either buying or selling a home. This is probably the biggest financial event of their lives – and probably the worst possible time for them to become a victim of identity theft. So, your job is to help prevent that!

I think most people believe that a thief needs a Social Security number or a credit card to steal someone's identity. Therefore it would be important to teach licensees/brokers that the thief only needs a little piece of information to create a whole new identity.

How do thieves steal an identity? One way identity theft starts is with the misuse of your personally identifying information such as your name and Social Security number, credit card numbers, or other financial account information. For identity thieves, this information is as good as gold. Skilled identity thieves may use a variety of methods to get your information, including:

1. **Dumpster Diving** - They rummage through trash looking for bills or other paper with your personal information on it.
2. **Skimming** - They steal credit/debit card numbers by using a special storage device when processing your card for a purchase.
3. **Phishing** - They pretend to be financial institutions or companies and send spam or pop-up messages to get you to reveal your personal information.
4. **Changing Your Address** - They divert your billing statements to another location by completing a change of address form.
5. **Old-Fashioned Stealing** - They steal wallets and purses; mail, including bank and credit card statements, pre-approved credit offers; and new checks or tax information. They steal personnel records, or bribe employees who have access.
6. **Pretexting** - They use false pretenses to obtain your personal information from financial institutions, telephone companies, and other sources.

Advise your customers to:

- Memorize their Social Security number and all passwords.
- Sign all new credit cards upon receipt, or write "ask for ID" on the signature line.
- Save all credit card receipts and match them against monthly bills to check for fraudulent purchases.
- Be aware of routine financial statements and call if they are not received on time.
- Notify credit card companies and financial institutions in advance of any change of address or phone number.
- Never loan your credit cards to anyone else.
- Report all lost or stolen credit cards immediately.
- Order a copy of your credit report annually.
- Always make Internet purchases through a secure website.
- Be wary of anyone calling to "confirm" personal information.
- When completing credit or loan applications, only list the last four digits of a credit card. Creditors only need to be able to match up what's on the credit report – they do not need the entire number.

Taking these steps is no guarantee that you will not be a victim of identity theft.

Preventative Measures

In a world where white-collar crime is rising, due partly to tremendous advances in technology, taking time to protect yourself will be time well spent.

"My life is in my wallet (or purse). What should I do?"

Answer: Preventive Measures

One simple way to protect yourself against identity theft is to limit the amount of confidential information you carry with you. I recommend that you not carry around bank account numbers, personal identification numbers (PINs), passports, birth certificates, and most importantly, Social Security cards. (Although many states continue to use Social Security numbers on drivers' licenses, this practice is changing.)

Avoid carrying more blank checks than you really need: a thief can cash checks or use them for purchases. A crook also can make use of the sensitive information pre-printed on your checks (your address, bank account number, even your telephone number). Many consumers even print their driver's license number or Social Security number on their checks. That's a definite no-no, because either number could help a thief apply for a loan, credit card or bank account in your name.

Keep good backup information about your accounts, just in case your wallet is lost or stolen. You'll want account numbers and phone numbers that can be used to report your losses or request new cards or emergency cash. Some people recommend photocopying your credit, debit, and ATM cards, as well as your driver's license and passport information.

Securely store any credit cards you don't really need or use. Among the reasons: A thief can dust off a "dormant" card and use card numbers and other personal information to make purchases or get a new card. You'll only find out about the problem when the collection notices arrive at your address. Cancelling the card will negatively impact your credit by lowering the total amount of available credit you have.

While it may seem obvious, it can't hurt to mention a few basic words about protecting your wallet: Don't take out your wallet until you actually need it, and don't forget your wallet before leaving a restaurant, store or any public place. And never put your wallet down alongside a cash register, in a phone booth or even on top of your car. A good rule of thumb is to always keep your hand on your wallet when it is out.

*Source: www.ftc.gov Identity Theft: What your customers should be aware of.

What To Do If You or Your Customer Becomes a Victim of Identity Theft

Share this information with any of your customers as soon as they discover that they are victims of identity theft:

First, contact local law enforcement.

Have them initiate a report for Fraudulent Use of Personal Identification. Get a copy of your police report or case number. Most credit card companies, banks, and others may ask you for it in order to make sure a crime has actually occurred.

Second, contact credit card issuers.

Close existing accounts and get replacement cards with new account numbers. Make sure to request that the old account reflect that it was "closed at consumer's request" for credit report purposes. It is also smart to follow up your telephone conversation with letters to the credit card companies that summarize your request in writing.

Request a change of PIN and new password on every existing credit, ATM or debit card.

Third, close any accounts the thief has opened in your name.

Ask your financial institutions to close all your accounts and reopen the accounts with passwords.

Fourth, contact fraud departments of the three major credit bureaus.

Report the theft of the credit cards and/or numbers. Ask that the accounts be flagged with a "fraud alert." This usually means that someone can't set up a new account in your name without the creditor calling you at a phone number you specify. Verify with the credit bureau representative you speak with that this will happen, and provide them with the number at which you want to be reached.

The down side of this is that you won't be able to get "instant credit" at stores when the cashier offers you an immediate discount if you open a credit card with that store. This flag, also known as a "victim's statement," is the best way to prevent unauthorized accounts.

Fifth, contact fraud departments of your credit card companies.

For each credit card that was compromised, you must contact the card company's customer service department and their fraud department. When you contact the fraud department, have them put a fraud alert on your account.

Everyday Technology & Social Media

"Social media should improve your life, not become your life!"

Patrick Driessen

Eight
Everyday Technology & Social Media

Technology is a great benefit to the real estate professional, but it can potentially increase your risks on the job.

Texting or talking on a cell phone, checking e-mail or transmitting documents on a PDA are all activities that require attention. As important as the activity seems to you at the time, isn't your life more important? The distraction of multitasking significantly decreases your awareness and marks you for an attacker as an easy target.

Cell Phones and PDAs

OK, so everyone loves talking on his cell phone, but did you know that doing it could be hazardous to your health? No, I'm not talking about the news reports you have heard that associate cell phone usage with brain tumors. I'm referring to the injuries that can result from talking on the cell phone while driving! There's no doubt about it: it's DANGEROUS! How many times have you seen another driver start to drift into another lane of traffic (maybe yours) and then when you look over at them what do you see? You got it, a cell phone!

They are more interested in their conversation than in obeying the rules of the road. Hard to believe, but cutting that big business deal or asking their spouse what to pick up at the grocery store becomes more important at that moment than their own safety.

Can you get a ticket for talking on a cell phone while driving, you ask? YES! Many countries as well as many cities and states across America have made it illegal to talk on a hand-held cell phone while driving. In states where there is no law against holding a cell phone while driving, police officers can ticket you for distracted driving. In other words, if you are doing something other than driving while driving (holding a cell phone, putting on lipstick, reading a map or book, etc.) and you are driving unsafely as a result of such activities, you may receive a ticket.

To make your day a little safer and your life a little easier, here are some cell phone safety tips:

- Try to place calls while your vehicle is stationary.
- Use a "hands-free" or speakerphone accessory. (These are available for most if not all hand-held cell phones.) Not only does this allow you to keep your hands on the wheel and your eyes on the road, but using a hands-free kit keeps the phone further from your head, reducing exposure to the alleged tumor-causing radiation.
- Never read or write text messages while driving. Taking your eyes off the road for a second or two

can result in a collision. Pull over to the side of the road if you must text.

- Program frequently called numbers into your phone's memory, allowing you to keep dialing to a minimum.
- If you must dial when the car is moving, hold the phone at eye level so you will have a clear view of the road.
- Make sure your phone is within easy reach while driving.
- Make sure 911 is programmed into your phone's memory should you need to report an accident or other emergency.
- Do not make emotional phone calls while driving (quitting your job, breaking up with a boyfriend or girlfriend, etc.), as you will be focused primarily on the call rather than your driving.
- Never read or write while the car is moving. If you must write a note or take down a phone number during a conversation, PULL OVER!
- Be careful when pulling over to place calls. To avoid being a crime victim, do not stop in dangerous areas and keep your car doors locked.
- If your phone is connected to your car's power source, disconnect your phone before using jumper cables. The power surge could damage your phone.

Safety Tips for Social Networking Sites

Social sites such as Facebook, My Space, Twitter, etc., are becoming more and more popular. But how do you protect yourself when on these largely open social sites?

Don't post information about yourself online that you don't want the whole world to know. The Internet is the world's biggest information exchange: many more people could see your information than you intend, including your employer, the police and strangers, some of whom could be dangerous.

Social networking sites have added a new factor to the "friends of friends" equation. By providing information about yourself and using blogs, chat rooms, e-mail, or instant messaging, you can communicate, either within a limited community, or with the world at large. But while the sites can increase your circle of friends, they also can increase your exposure to people who have less-than-friendly intentions. You've heard the stories about people who were stalked by someone they met online, had their identity stolen, or had their computer hacked.

Tips for socializing safely online:

- Think about how different sites work before deciding to join a site. Some sites will allow only a defined community of users to access posted content; others allow anyone and everyone to view postings.
- Think about keeping some control over the information you post. Consider restricting access

to your page to a select group of people, for example, your friends, your team, your community groups, or your family.

- Keep your personal information to yourself. Don't post your Social Security number, address, home phone number, or bank and credit card account numbers — and don't post other people's information, either. Be cautious about posting information that could be used to locate you offline.
- In dating sites, make sure your screen name doesn't say too much about you. Don't use your full name, your age, or the part of town where you live. Even if you think your screen name makes you anonymous, it may not take a genius to combine clues to figure out who you are and where you can be found.
- Post only information that you are comfortable with others seeing (and knowing) about you. Many people can see your page.
- Remember that once you post information online, you can't take it back. Even if you delete the information from a site, older versions exist on other people's computers.
- Consider your photo. It can be altered and broadcast in ways you may not be happy about. If you do post one, ask yourself whether it's one you would display in the living room.
- Flirting with strangers online could have serious consequences. Because some people lie about who they really are, you never really know who you're dealing with.

- Be wary if a new online friend wants to meet you in person. Before you decide to meet someone, do your research! See what background you can dig up through online search engines. If you decide to meet them, be smart about it! Meet in a public place, during the day, with friends you trust. Tell someone where you're going, and when you expect to be back.
- Trust your gut if you have suspicions. If you feel threatened by someone or uncomfortable because of something online, tell someone you trust and report it to the police and the social networking site. You could end up preventing someone else from becoming a victim.

A Word about Firearms

"To disarm the people…was the best and most effectual way to enslave them."

George Mason

"On average 3 children died every day in non-homicide firearm incidents from 2000-2005."

Centers for Disease Control

Bonus
A Word about Firearms

Firearms are as American as apple pie. It is estimated that two out of three homes in America have a firearm.

Firearm safety is important to everyone. No one wants handgun accidents to happen yet they do everyday. Just the mention of the word firearms and you will get a strong reaction from both sides. While I am not here to debate the firearms issue, my request to you is simple. If you are going to have a firearm in your home, there are some simple rules.

1. Become legal and learn the firearms laws that apply to your state.
2. It is important to become thoroughly familiar with your weapon.

The National Rifle Association has a great program called The Eddie Eagle GunSafe® Program that teaches children in pre-K through third grade four important steps to take if they find a gun. These steps are presented by the program's mascot, Eddie Eagle®, in an easy-to-remember format consisting of the following simple rules:

If you see a gun:

- STOP!
- Don't Touch.
- Leave the Area.
- Tell an Adult.

The next step in becoming skillful in handling handguns is using the safety knowledge that you have acquired.

Six basic gun safety rules for gun owners to understand and practice at all times:

1. Treat all guns as if they are loaded.
2. Keep the gun pointed in the safest possible direction.
3. Keep your finger off the trigger until you are ready to shoot.
4. Know your target, its surroundings and beyond.
5. Know how to properly operate your gun.
6. Store your gun safely and securely to prevent unauthorized use.

1. Treat all guns as if they are loaded.

- Always assume that a gun is loaded, even if you think it is unloaded.
- Every time a gun is handled for any reason, check to see that it is unloaded. For specific instructions on how to unload a handgun, see the following section.
- If you are unable to check a gun to see if it is unloaded, leave it alone and seek help from someone more knowledgeable about guns.

2. Keep the gun pointed in the safest direction possible.

- Always be aware of where the gun is pointing. A "safe direction" is one where an accidental discharge of the gun will not cause injury or damage.
- Only point a gun at an object that you intend to shoot.
- Never point a gun toward yourself or another person.

3. Keep your finger off the trigger until you are ready to shoot.

- Always keep your finger off the trigger and outside the trigger guard until you are ready to shoot.
- Even though it may be comfortable to rest your finger on the trigger, it also is unsafe.
- If you are moving around with your finger on the trigger and stumble or fall, you could inadvertently pull the trigger.
- Sudden loud noises or movements can result in an accidental discharge because there is a natural tendency to tighten the muscles when startled.
- The trigger is for firing, the handle is for handling.

4. Know your target and what is beyond.

- Check that the areas in front of and behind your target are safe before shooting.

- Be aware that if the bullet misses or completely passes through the target, it could strike a person or object.
- Identify the target and make sure it is what you intend to shoot. If you are in doubt, DON'T SHOOT!
- Never fire at a target that is only a movement, color, sound or unidentifiable shape.
- Be aware of all the people around you before you shoot.

5. Know how to properly use your gun.

- It is important to become thoroughly familiar with your gun. You should know its mechanical characteristics including how to properly load, unload and clear a malfunction from your gun.
- Obviously, not all guns are mechanically the same. Never assume that what applies to one make or model is exactly applicable to another.
- You should direct questions regarding the operation of your gun to your firearms dealer, or contact the manufacturer directly.

6. Store you gun safety and securely.

- When the gun is not in your hands, you must still think of safety.

- Use an approved firearms safety device on the gun, such as a trigger lock or cable lock, so it cannot be fired.
- Store it unloaded in a locked container, such as an approved lock box or a gun safe.
- Store your gun in a different location than the ammunition.
- For maximum safety you should use both a locking device and a storage container.

About the Author

Andrew Wooten is the president of Safety Awareness Firearms Education (S.A.F.E.), and has been in the safety and security industry since 1984, providing safety programs internationally. He provides practical advice about security, crime, loss prevention, and avoiding liability. His main office is located near Jacksonville, Florida.

Mr. Wooten has over 26 years of education, training, and experience in crime prevention and security management and has earned many professional certifications in his field. He has conducted over 4,000 training programs worldwide. Mr. Wooten is considered to be an expert in the fields of safety and security, and crime and loss prevention, and specializes in the anticipation, recognition, and prevention of crime on most property types. He is available to consult with business owners, managers, insurance agencies; Mr. Wooten will also consult with the media, attorneys, and testify as a security expert witness.

Mr. Wooten is an internationally known author, trainer, and speaker. He is often asked to speak at conferences and corporate seminars. He has consulted with or appeared on many radio and television shows.

Experience

In addition to his formal education and experience, Mr. Wooten has absorbed thousands of hours of specialized training. Throughout his career, he has developed cost-effective security programs to protect small, medium, and large commercial properties as well as several world-renowned corporations. He has thousands of hours of hands-on experience working against the folks who commit crime against property and person.

S.A.F.E has earned a solid reputation for conceiving solutions that are practical, reasonable and effective. It's Mr. Wooten's hands-on approach; investigating client locations in-depth in addition to listening to clients explain what they perceive as security issues that allow him to design the best programs and security systems. The program design and implementation must complement and protect the client's assets.

Mr. Wooten holds a Bachelor of Science degree in Business Administration.

Professional Licenses & Certifications

- Crime Prevention Practitioner (CPP)
- Workplace Violence Trainer (WVT)
- Convenience Store Inspector (CSI)
- Victim Services Practitioner (VCP)
- Basic Crime Practitioner (BCP)
- Advance Crime Practitioner (ACP)
- Residential Crime Practitioner (RCP)
- Commercial Crime Practitioner (CCP)

Professional Memberships

- American Society for Industrial Security

- International Society of Crime Prevention Practitioners
- International CPTED Association
- National Rifle Association
- Society for Human Resource Management (SHRM)
- American Society for Industrial Security (ASIS)
- Attorney General of Florida (Crime Prevention Practitioner)
- Department of Justice
- National Sheriff's Association
- National Speakers Association

Mr. Wooten's philosophy and golden rule is that, "A person's best weapon is themselves: their mind, voice and body." Each person, regardless of size, is capable of learning and adapting some form of the techniques presented in his seminars.

Appendix One: Simple Steps for Safeguarding Your Office

By now, you are aware of potential dangers that you face when you are meeting clients, showing properties or hosting open houses, and in your car. There is one more place to consider: the office where you work.

You can help safeguard your business's (and your personal) property, and the safety of all who work in the office, with a few procedures and precautions:

1. Know staff in other nearby businesses and be aware of their schedules.
2. Ensure that all doors other than the main entrance are secured.
3. Make certain windows are not obscured so that passersby can see in.
4. Make sure there is a clear exit route from the service desk to the door.
5. Never allow visitors to wander freely about the business. Have the person whom they want to see come to the front office area and escort the individual to the meeting area.
6. Have a visitor log book and policy on issuing visitor tags that limit access to certain areas and hours of the day.
7. If you encounter an individual while working late or alone, indicate to that person that you are not alone. Say something like, "My supervisor will be right with you and should be able to assist you."

8. Keep personal information private. When in front of customers, new coworkers or anyone in general with whom you are not comfortable avoid discussing where you live, and after-work or vacation plans.
9. Install a spare phone in the storage room.
10. Install an alarm, (preferably both audible and monitored). Have alarm buttons in strategic spots; i.e. panic buttons at the reception area.
11. Install surveillance cameras that will monitor the front entrance, the reception area, and other areas that are accessible to the public.

(Source: Sonoma County Crime Crushers)

Appendix Two: Answers to "What Would You Do?"

Chapter One: What Would You Do?

Scenario 1:

You're working an open house when a middle-aged man and his wife show up to see the home. The following day, they call you and ask to see more homes. After you meet them at a home, they ask if you'll come to their home to assess its value. The possibility of a new listing intrigues you.

As you walk through their home, something doesn't feel right to you, but you can't put your finger on what it is. Everything seems to be in order, so you decide you're just being paranoid. They direct you toward the upstairs bedroom next. What would you do?

a. Dismiss your fears as unimportant (after all, the wife is there), and go on into the bedroom with the couple.
b. Pretend like you have just received a call and must step outside to take the call.
c. Call your buddy and ask him/her to meet you there ASAP before proceeding any further.
d. Don't go by yourself in the first place.

Answer: d, but if you are already there, answer c.

Scenario 2:

You're a new agent who's been working the phones, and a man calls and asks to see some properties. You meet the client and you proceed to show him several properties. You find it a bit odd that he spends extra time in the smaller bedrooms and he explains he'll have part-time custody of his children. But something just doesn't seem right about his behavior. What would you do?

a. Never have taken him to see any properties by yourself. You should have met him in your office and had him complete a Prospect Identification Form and gotten a copy of his driver's license.
b. Excuse yourself to take a call, and call your office once outside to ask them to run a check on this prospect's phone number.
c. Continue showing him properties; after all, you really need to make a sale, and everybody has their quirks.
d. Jot down the license plate number on his vehicle and pay closer attention to his actions at the next property you show him.

Answer: a

Scenario 3:

You get a call from a prospect who says he's at a property you've listed and would like to see it. Business has been slow lately. You're not far from the address, so you agree to meet him there. When you arrive at the property, you find not only your prospect and his wife, but also a second man with him. You're a little apprehensive about this, but you are reassured by the other women's presence. What would you do?

a. Go on into the house with the three people, reassured by the presence of a woman.
b. Call someone from your buddy list and have a buddy meet you around the corner from the property, so both of you arrive together. Then have your buddy call your office and talk with someone, making sure the prospects hear your buddy say where you are and what you're about to do.
c. Pretend to call your office and talk with someone, making sure the prospects hear you say that the other person is on their way there and will arrive within a few minutes.
d. Pretend that you have received a phone call from your broker and an emergency has come up. You explain that you won't be able to show them the property until you return to your office first. You apologize; get back into your car, promising to return within the hour, inviting them to wait for you there.

Answer: You should not have gone by yourself in the first place, so at this time you should do b, c and/or d.

Chapter Two: What Would You Do?

Scenario 1

You consistently receive an extremely higher number of phone calls at your office for showings and listings, much higher than other agents in your office. E-mails from your website are also numerous. However, most of these calls and e-mails never materialize into sales. You consistently have a high number of no-shows at the office for appointments that you have made. When you are conducting an open house, your traffic is extremely high, however your sales are far below everyone else in your office. What are the areas you need to look at?

a. Your closing technique.
b. Where you are advertising your open houses.
c. The photograph of you that appears in your ads.
d. Your telephone technique.

Answer: c

Scenario 2

You arrive at a home a prospect has requested to see. This is an unfamiliar neighborhood to you but it looks nice and quiet. As you go to open the lock box, you feel a cold shiver up your spine but dismiss it as nerves. Once inside the house you begin to do a walk through, looking for interesting things to point out to your clients. All of a sudden you get an uneasy feeling. You cannot pinpoint why, but something doesn't feel right. What should you do now?

a. Dismiss your feeling, what could possibly be wrong?
b. Call your buddy list and use your pre-determined distress code.
c. Lock the house and leave immediately until someone on your buddy list can join you at the house.
d. Call 911.

Answer: b and c

Scenario 3

You've recently become engaged. Your fiancé surprised you with the most beautiful diamond you've ever seen! You promised him that you'd never take it off. This afternoon, you are meeting a new client in the office. He's an attractive man who appears to be single, and was quite flirty with you over the phone. You want to establish a professional relationship with him so that you can sell him a house. What's the safest way to do that?

a. Make sure the photograph of you with your fiancé is well in view during your meeting in the office.
b. Show off that gorgeous diamond on your left hand.

c. Refer to your fiancé often in your conversation with the client.
d. Don't be alone with him in the office and introduce him to others.

Answer: a and d

Scenario 4

This is the busiest day you've had in a long time, and boy, is it welcomed! After dropping your daughter off at school, you have to meet a couple at your office, and then show them a few homes before a luncheon meeting with the local Chamber of Commerce. After the luncheon, you're sitting at an open house for two hours, and then you must head back to the office to meet a new client and assess his needs. Next, you have more homes to show a couple you've been working with for a few months. Finally, you need to stop by and pick up a signature on a new listing on your way home. What should you do before each of the stops in your busy day?

a. Check your voicemail to see if there are any calls you need to return.
b. Call your buddy to let her know where you are going and with whom.
c. Check in with the office receptionist.
d. Update your status on Twitter.

Answer: b, c and d

Chapter Three: What Would You Do?

Scenario 1:

The husband half of a couple to whom you've been showing several houses calls you on a Saturday afternoon and says he's at one of the houses you've shown them before. He says his wife was called into work, and he can't remember whether it was this house or another that had the nice workshop off the garage. He would like to take a quick look again. The family that lives in the home now is not at home. Can you meet him there and show him the garage?

a. Tell him you can meet him. Call your buddy list and have someone go with you. Then when you and your buddy are on your way, call your broker.
b. Tell him you're currently showing property to someone else and offer to meet him in an hour at your office.
c. Tell him you're unable to meet today, and suggest that you meet in your office tomorrow, when his wife is available. Then you can review all the details of the houses you've shown them.
d. Tell him you'll be there in half an hour, and then head out to show him the house again.

Answer: a

Scenario 2:

You're setting up your home office, and look forward to being able to get some work done there without having to go into your broker's office. Which of the following is an element you need to include in your home office?

a. Workspace with desk, chair and sufficient lighting
b. Secure wireless Internet access
c. A secure filing system for your customers' paperwork
d. A reception area for customers

Answer: a, b and c

Scenario 3:

While working at an open house where traffic is slow, you're using your laptop to check and respond to e-mails. You're in the middle of typing a response to a client when someone shows up to see the house. What would you do?

a. Close your laptop and leave it on the desk where you were sitting while you show them the house.
b. Leave your laptop as you were working on it and show them the house.
c. Tell them to look around while you finish, and you'll be with them in a few minutes; take the time to close your laptop and secure it.

d. Ask them to have a seat for a moment while you finish, and hand them a flyer about the house to look at while you close your laptop and secure it.

Answer: c

Chapter 5: What Would You Do?

Scenario 1

You are walking to your car from the office after dark, regretting that the only parking place earlier in the day had been near some bushes at the far end of the lot. Suddenly, a feeling comes over you that something is not right. Glancing around, you don't see anything out of the ordinary, and there appears to be no one else around. As you approach your car, a man springs out of the bushes, shows what appears to be a knife, and screams, "Gimme the purse!" What would you do?

a. Wet your pants.
b. Put your hands out in front of you and yell, "Stop!"
c. Throw your purse as far away from your car as you can, and when he runs to get it, quickly unlock your car, get in and immediately lock the doors and call 911.
d. Toss your purse to him, while backing away and you should have been talking to someone on the phone as you were walking. (Remember what Andrew said.)

Answer: d

Scenario 2

On your way into the office at six-thirty in the morning, you stop by to pick up some donuts for your clients who are coming in to sign some papers on their way to work. As you walk back across the parking lot to your car, you can see that in the few minutes you were away, someone has smashed a window and stolen your GPS system. What would you do?

a. Call your clients and tell them you'll be a little late.
b. Go back into the donut shop, where there are other people, and call 911 on your cell phone.
c. Curse at yourself for not putting the GPS system into the glove box, like Andrew told you to do.
d. Look around to see if the thief is still in sight and chase after him as you call 911 on your cell phone.

Answer: b and c

Chapter 6: What Would You Do?

Scenario 1

You've been working with a client for a few months and he just can't seem to find the right house, although you've shown him several that meet the needs he described to you. He calls you one day and wants to meet you at a house in a new development on the outskirts of town. He even gives you the directions to get there and seems very interested in this house. He wants to see it as soon as possible. You make an appointment with him for later in the afternoon, and then head over there to preview the house.

You have some trouble finding it, as the development is so new your GPS unit doesn't seem to have those streets on it yet and the directions he gave you seem to lead nowhere.

This development is so far out in the woods, you can't even get much of a signal on your cell phone. As you're driving through the development looking for the house, you notice a car just like your client's parked around the corner from where you finally locate the house. What would you do?

a. Park in the driveway of the house and start looking for a unique feature to mention to your client.
b. Park on the street in front of the house, call your buddy to give your location, and begin your preview activities.

c. Call someone on your buddy list and have them meet you. Don't meet the client until your buddy arrives.
d. Leave the area immediately and call your client to say that something's come up and you won't be able to show him the house this afternoon. Reschedule the appointment for another day.

Answer: c (The best option would have been not to go alone in the first place. Take a buddy with you.)

Scenario 2

When you arrive to preview a house in a very upscale neighborhood, you find a dense privacy hedge planted across the front of the property so that the entrance to the house is not visible from the street.

The driveway goes past the side of the house, passing under a large porte-cochere by the side door on the way to the garage in the rear. Several mature trees and lush flower beds grace the front yard, while the back yard is filled with pathways, vine-laden arbors, and even a carp pond.

You notice more thick hedges planted near the front door that make it a very narrow entrance for a house of this size. When you return with your clients, how will you safely unlock the front door of the house without leaving yourself vulnerable to attack?

a. Ask the clients to wait in the car until you can get the front door open for them.
b. Direct clients to have a look at the porte-cochere, and while they are doing so, you unlock the front door.
c. Make note of the landscaping in the front yard and ask the clients to take a closer look at it; while they are doing so, you unlock the front door.
d. Hand the clients the key and have them unlock the front door while you wait behind them.

Answer: b and c

Scenario 3

A prospect who says they were referred to you by one of your Chamber of Commerce contacts calls on a Saturday morning and asks you about a house she's just spotted, and she wants to see it immediately.

Remembering your safety training, you ask her to meet you at a nearby Starbuck's. She explains that she's going through a divorce and needs to find a house quickly.

But when you ask to see her driver's license, she gets nervous and says she'd left it at home when she changed purses that morning. What would you do?

a. Tell her you're sorry, but your broker insists that you can't show a house to anyone without a photo ID. Make an appointment for her to stop by the office on Monday, when you can get the proper paperwork completed to show her the house.
b. Never show an empty home alone, always take a buddy.
c. Call your buddy. Pretend that you're talking to your broker and discuss, in the client's earshot, how he's going to meet you at the house in fifteen minutes. Then agree to head over to the house with the client, with the understanding that your broker (actually, your buddy) will be arriving soon.
d. Have the prospect complete a Prospect Identification Form, then call your buddy to relay the information while you're sitting at Starbuck's, so the client can hear you. Wait a few minutes for a call back to confirm that the information is valid, watching to see if the prospect backs down from seeing the house now, just in case the information she gave you is phony.

Answer: b and c

Scenario 4

You've been working an open house all afternoon and it's getting late in the day. You think everyone has left, but as you're making the rounds to lock up, you find a man who had come by earlier during a rush of people. You'd thought he'd left with them, but he's been lurking in one of the upstairs rooms. He pulls out a gun and tells you he's glad to catch you alone. What would you do?

a. Tell him your broker is due to stop by any minute.
b. Look around for something you can use to counterattack him.
c. Ask him what he wants, and make your choice to fight back or not fight back, either option is right as long as you are making the decision.
d. Put your hands out in front of you and yell, "Stop!"

Answer: a, b and c

Appendix Three: Contact Information

Equifax, Inc.
P.O. Box 105496
Atlanta, GA 30348-5496
888-766-0008 (Fraud Hotline)
800-685-1111(Report Order)
www.equifax.com

Experian
P.O. Box 2104
Allen, Texas 75013-2104
888-397-3742(Fraud Hotline)
800-685-1111(Report Order)
www.experian.com

Trans Union
Fraud Victim Assistance Department
P.O. Box 390
Springfield, PA 19064-0390
800-680-7289 (Fraud Hotline)
800-916-8800 (Report Order)
www.transunion.com

Federal Trade Commission
600 Pennsylvania Ave, NW
Washington, DC 20580
Toll-free 877-FTC-HELP (382-4357)
www.ftc.gov/ftc/complaint.htm

S.A.F.E.
4940 Emerson St.
Suite 103
Jacksonville, FL 32207
(904) 398-1848
www.justbesafe.com

Appendix Four: "The List"

"The List" comes from the book, *Mentor: The Kid and The* CEO by Tom Pace. "The List" is suggestions on how to live your life to its fullest extent. I truly believe you cannot succeed in life without helping others. If you practice "The List" not only will you become a better person but your actions will change others for the better too.

1. Finish what you start.
2. Have integrity.
3. Have values.
4. Be a mentor.
5. Stay committed.
6. Listen well.
7. Don't take things personally.
8. Give away a book.
9. Open doors for people.
10. Help others.
11. Ask questions.
12. Encourage others.
13. Move someone for free.
14. Take action.
15. Pick up trash.
16. Be cheerful.
17. Write a book.
18. Be kind.
19. Save 10 percent.
20. Visit someone in the hospital.
21. Visit someone in treatment.
22. Believe in yourself.

23. Have a dream list.
24. Use a to-do list.
25. Don't worry.
26. Visit someone in jail.
27. Ideas. Action. Commitment.
28. Visit someone in a homeless shelter.
29. Buy someone dinner.
30. Exercise.
31. Take vitamins.
32. Have sympathy.
33. Winners take action.
34. Share hope.
35. Dream big.
36. Winners plan.
37. Call a friend.
38. Planners win.
39. Learn from other people.
40. Do good.
41. Use good manners.
42. Call a relative.
43. Have fun.
44. Become a champion.
45. Repay favors.
46. Don't assume anything.
47. Always be on time.
48. Go to a seminar.
49. Take a walk.
50. Go to the park.
51. Finish strong.
52. Read.
53. Sharing is caring.
54. Don't blame others.
55. Focus.

56. Exercise your mind.
57. Be slow to anger.
58. Be honest.
59. Give freely.
60. Creation, not competition.
61. Do important things first.
62. Carry a book with you.
63. Always do your best.
64. Develop routine.
65. Drink water.
66. Accept responsibility.
67. Stick to your plan.
68. Invite someone to church.
69. Enjoy church.
70. Be a greeter at church.
71. Run four days a week.
72. Reconciliation, not retaliation.
73. Be a person of value.
74. Value people.
75. Be loyal.
76. Say what you mean.
77. Miracles happen.
78. Give back.
79. Believe in others.
80. Impact the lives of others.
81. Mean what you say.
82. Read more.
83. Be polite.
84. Accept challenges.
85. Defeat challenges
86. Get a mentor.
87. Be a friend.
88. Keep your promises.

89. Be kind.
90. Go the extra mile.
91. Be frugal.
92. Thank people.
93. Use positive words.
94. Remember your victories.
95. What gets measured gets improved.
96. Learn. Teach. Do
97. Enjoy new things.
98. Be social.
99. Share good news.
100. Encourage others.
101. Avoid self-doubt.
102. Play by the rules.
103. Use kind words.
104. Don't always talk about yourself.
105. Share in other people's joy.
106. Concentrate.
107. Dishonesty costs everything.
108. Motivate yourself.
109. Be real.
110. Seek understanding.
111. Become wise.
112. Use your talents.
113. Everyone needs help.
114. Everyone suffers.
115. Always take action.
116. Don't run from challenges.
117. Make a difference.
118. Have faith.
119. Give back.
120. Teach others.
121. With action great things will happen.

122. Significant people recognize significant actions.
123. Appreciate your life.
124. Do Yoga.
125. Yoga is cool.

Made in the USA
Lexington, KY
16 December 2014